Election Reform,
Second Edition

Affirmative Action

Amateur Athletics

American Military Policy

Animal Rights

Bankruptcy Law

Blogging

Capital Punishment,
Second Edition

Disaster Relief

DNA Evidence

Educational Standards

Election Reform, Second Edition

Energy Policy

Environmental Regulations
and Global Warming

The FCC and
Regulating Indecency

Fetal Rights

Food Safety

Freedom of Speech

Gay Rights

Gun Control

Hate Crimes

Immigrants' Rights After 9/11

Immigration Policy,
Second Edition

The Internet and Crime

Juvenile Justice

Legalizing Marijuana,
Second Edition

Mandatory Military Service

Media Bias

Mental Health Reform

Miranda Rights

Open Government

Physician-Assisted Suicide

Policing the Internet

Prescription and
Non-prescription Drugs

Prisoners' Rights

Private Property Rights

Product Liability

Protecting Ideas

Racial Profiling

Regulating Violence
in Entertainment

Religion in Public Schools

Reproductive Rights

The Right to Die

The Right to Privacy

Rights of Students,
Second Edition

Search and Seizure

Smoking Bans, Second Edition

Stem Cell Research and Cloning

Tort Reform

Trial of Juveniles as Adults

Unions and Labor Laws

Universal Healthcare

The War on Terror,
Second Edition

Welfare Reform

White-Collar Crime

Women in the Military

Election Reform,
Second Edition

Alan Marzilli, M.A., J.D.

SERIES EDITOR
Alan Marzilli, M.A., J.D.

CHELSEA HOUSE
PUBLISHERS

An imprint of Infobase Publishing

Election Reform, Second Edition

Copyright © 2011 by Infobase Publishing

All rights reserved. No part of this book may be reproduced or utilized in any form or by any means, electronic or mechanical, including photocopying, recording, or by any information storage or retrieval systems, without permission in writing from the publisher. For information, contact:

Chelsea House
An imprint of Infobase Publishing
132 West 31st Street
New York, NY 10001

Library of Congress Cataloging-in-Publication Data
Marzilli, Alan.
  Election reform / by Alan Marzilli.— 2nd ed.
  p. cm. — (Point/counterpoint)
  Includes bibliographical references and index.
  ISBN 978-1-60413-691-3 (hardcover)
  1. Elections—United States—Juvenile literature. 2. Election law—United States—Juvenile literature. 3. Political campaigns—United States—Juvenile literature. 4. Campaign funds—United States—Juvenile literature. 5. Political participation—United States—Juvenile literature. I. Title. II. Series.
  JK1978.M37 2010
  324.6'30973—dc22
                                    2009051401

Chelsea House books are available at special discounts when purchased in bulk quantities for businesses, associations, institutions, or sales promotions. Please call our Special Sales Department in New York at (212) 967-8800 or (800) 322-8755.

You can find Chelsea House on the World Wide Web at http://www.chelseahouse.com.

Text design by Keith Trego
Cover design by Alicia Post
Composition by EJB Publishing Services
Cover printed by Bang Printing, Brainerd, MN
Book printed and bound by Bang Printing, Brainerd, MN
Date printed: October 2010
Printed in the United States of America

10 9 8 7 6 5 4 3 2 1

This book is printed on acid-free paper.

All links and Web addresses were checked and verified to be correct at the time of publication. Because of the dynamic nature of the Web, some addresses and links may have changed since publication and may no longer be valid.

Foreword   **6**

INTRODUCTION
Voting: The Cornerstone of Democracy?   **11**

POINT
Voting Rights Require Strong Protections   **21**

COUNTERPOINT
Strict Registration Requirements Prevent Fraud   **34**

POINT
Money Corrupts American Democracy   **45**

COUNTERPOINT
Campaign Contributions Are Political Speech   **58**

POINT
Regulating Television Promotes Fair Campaigns   **69**

COUNTERPOINT
Regulating Television Is Unconstitutional
and Undemocratic   **81**

CONCLUSION
The Future of American Democracy   **92**

Appendix: Beginning Legal Research   **103**
Elements of the Argument   **106**
Notes   **108**
Resources   **111**
Picture Credits   **114**
Index   **115**

Alan Marzilli, M.A., J.D.
Birmingham, Alabama

The POINT/COUNTERPOINT series offers the reader a greater understanding of some of the most controversial issues in contemporary
American society—issues such as capital punishment, immigration,
gay rights, and gun control. We have looked for the most contemporary issues and have included topics—such as the controversies
surrounding "blogging"—that we could not have imagined when the
series began.

In each volume, the author has selected an issue of particular
importance and set out some of the key arguments on both sides of the
issue. Why study both sides of the debate? Maybe you have yet to make
up your mind on an issue, and the arguments presented in the book
will help you to form an opinion. More likely, however, you will already
have an opinion on many of the issues covered by the series. There is
always the chance that you will change your opinion after reading the
arguments for the other side. But even if you are firmly committed to
an issue—for example, school prayer or animal rights—reading both
sides of the argument will help you to become a more effective advo-
cate for your cause. By gaining an understanding of opposing arguments, you can develop answers to those arguments.

Perhaps more importantly, listening to the other side sometimes
helps you see your opponent's arguments in a more human way. For
example, Sister Helen Prejean, one of the nation's most visible opponents of capital punishment, has been deeply affected by her interac-
tions with the families of murder victims. By seeing the families' grief
and pain, she understands much better why people support the death
penalty, and she is able to carry out her advocacy with a greater sensi-
tivity to the needs and beliefs of death penalty supporters.

The books in the series include numerous features that help the
reader to gain a greater understanding of the issues. Real-life examples
illustrate the human side of the issues. Each chapter also includes
excerpts from relevant laws, court cases, and other material, which
provide a better foundation for understanding the arguments. The

volumes contain citations to relevant sources of law and information, and an appendix guides the reader through the basics of legal research, both on the Internet and in the library. Today, through free Web sites, it is easy to access legal documents, and these books might give you ideas for your own research.

Studying the issues covered by the POINT/COUNTERPOINT series is more than an academic activity. The issues described in the books affect all of us as citizens. They are the issues that today's leaders debate and tomorrow's leaders will decide. While all of the issues covered in the POINT/COUNTERPOINT series are controversial today, and will remain so for the foreseeable future, it is entirely possible that the reader might one day play a central role in resolving the debate. Today it might seem that some debates—such as capital punishment and abortion—will never be resolved.

However, our nation's history is full of debates that seemed as though they never would be resolved, and many of the issues are now well settled—at least on the surface. In the nineteenth century, abolitionists met with widespread resistance to their efforts to end slavery. Ultimately, the controversy threatened the union, leading to the Civil War between the northern and southern states. Today, while a public debate over the merits of slavery would be unthinkable, racism persists in many aspects of society.

Similarly, today nobody questions women's right to vote. Yet at the beginning of the twentieth century, suffragists fought public battles for women's voting rights, and it was not until the passage of the Nineteenth Amendment in 1920 that the legal right of women to vote was established nationwide.

What makes an issue controversial? Often, controversies arise when most people agree that there is a problem but disagree about the best way to solve it. There is little argument that poverty is a major problem in the United States, especially in inner cities and rural areas. Yet, people disagree vehemently about the best way to address the problem. To some, the answer is social programs, such as welfare, food stamps, and public housing. However, many argue that such subsidies encourage dependence on government benefits while unfairly penalizing those who work and pay taxes, and that the real solution is to require people to support themselves.

American society is in a constant state of change, and sometimes modern practices clash with what many consider to be "traditional values," which are often rooted in conservative political views or religious beliefs. Many blame high crime rates, and problems such as poverty, illiteracy, and drug use on the breakdown of the traditional family structure of a married mother and father raising their children. Since the "sexual revolution" of the 1960s and 1970s, sparked in part by the widespread availability of the birth control pill, marriage rates have declined, and the number of children born outside of marriage has increased. The sexual revolution led to controversies over birth control, sex education, and other issues, most prominently abortion. Similarly, the gay rights movement has been challenged as a threat to traditional values. While many gay men and lesbians want to have the same right to marry and raise families as heterosexuals, many politicians and others have challenged gay marriage and adoption as a threat to American society.

Sometimes, new technology raises issues that we have never faced before, and society disagrees about the best solution. Are people free to swap music online, or does this violate the copyright laws that protect songwriters and musicians' ownership of the music that they create? Should scientists use "genetic engineering" to create new crops that are resistant to disease and pests and produce more food, or is it too risky to use a laboratory to create plants that nature never intended? Modern medicine has continued to increase the average lifespan—which is now 77 years, up from under 50 years at the beginning of the twentieth century—but many people are now choosing to die in comfort rather than living with painful ailments in their later years. For doctors, this presents an ethical dilemma: should they allow their patients to die? Should they assist patients in ending their own lives painlessly?

Perhaps the most controversial issues are those that implicate a Constitutional right. The Bill of Rights—the first 10 Amendments to the U.S. Constitution—spells out some of the most fundamental rights that distinguish our democracy from other nations with fewer freedoms. However, the sparsely worded document is open to interpretation, with each side saying that the Constitution is on their side. The Bill of Rights was meant to protect individual liberties; however, the needs of some individuals clash with society's needs. Thus, the Constitution often serves as a battleground between individuals and government officials seeking to protect society in some way. The First Amendment's guarantee of "freedom of speech" leads to some very difficult questions. Some forms of expression—such as burning an American flag—lead to public outrage, but are protected by the First Amendment. Other types of expression that most people find objectionable—such as child pornography—are not protected by the Constitution. The question is not only where to draw the line, but whether drawing lines around constitutional rights threatens our liberty.

The Bill of Rights raises many other questions about individual rights and societal "good." Is a prayer before a high school football game an "establishment of religion" prohibited by the First Amendment? Does the Second Amendment's promise of "the right to bear arms" include concealed handguns? Does stopping and frisking someone standing on a known drug corner constitute "unreasonable search and seizure" in violation of the Fourth Amendment? Although the U.S. Supreme Court has the ultimate authority in interpreting the U.S. Constitution, its answers do not always satisfy the public. When a group of nine people—sometimes by a five-to-four vote—makes a decision that affects hundreds of millions of others, public outcry can be expected. For example, the Supreme Court's 1973 ruling in *Roe v. Wade* that abortion is protected by the Constitution did little to quell the debate over abortion.

Whatever the root of the controversy, the books in the POINT/ COUNTERPOINT series seek to explain to the reader the origins of the debate, the current state of the law, and the arguments on either side of the debate. Our hope in creating this series is that readers will be better informed about the issues facing not only our politicians, but all of our nation's citizens, and become more actively involved in resolving these debates, as voters, concerned citizens, journalists, or maybe even elected officials.

This volume examines an issue at the heart of American democracy: voting. Americans have fought hard to ensure that most adults have the right to vote. Over the past two centuries, amendments to the U.S. Constitution have extended the right to vote to former slaves, women, and 18-year-olds. The year 2008 saw a day that many thought would never come—the election of an African-American president.

Yet today, the question remains: Does every vote count? The disputed 2000 election, for example, shook the nation's faith in the electoral system. In one of the tightest races in American history, Florida election workers created a national controversy by turning voters away and disqualifying many of the ballots cast. Ultimately, the U.S. Supreme Court rejected Vice President Al Gore's challenge, declaring Governor George W. Bush of Texas to be the elected president. No similar controversy existed in 2004 or 2008, but many raised questions during the 2008 election about the voter registration tactics of ACORN, a grassroots organization tied to the Obama campaign.

Since the first edition of this book was written, there have been new laws and new U.S. Supreme Court decisions, but many of the same controversies remain. How can we limit the influence of money on elections? How should campaign advertisements be regulated? What can be done to protect every eligible voter's right to cast a ballot?

Voting: The Cornerstone of Democracy?

The 2008 presidential election was history in the making. With Barack Obama and Joe Biden facing John McCain and Sarah Palin, U.S. voters would for the first time ever elect someone other than a white man to either the presidency or the vice presidency. In the wake of President Obama's victory, supporters pointed to record voter turnout as an indicator that America was ready to support a candidate regardless of the color of his (or her) skin. According to the U.S. Census Bureau, 5 million more people voted in 2008 than in 2004. This number included 2 million more African-American voters, 2 million more Hispanic voters, and 600,000 more Asian voters.[1]

It is important, however, to consider these numbers in the context of overall voter turnout. According to census figures, although 90 percent of registered voters cast their votes, a significant number of voting-age Americans were not registered to vote. In fact, fewer than half of Hispanic and Asian adults voted, while just under two-thirds of African-American and non-Hispanic white adults voted. More surprisingly, while President Obama had generated widespread enthusiasm and support by using technology such as Facebook and Twitter, fewer than half of adults aged 18 to 24 voted in the election.

There are many reasons people do not register and vote. For example, people serving prison sentences or on probation are generally restricted from voting. Many people, however, simply do not bother to register, perhaps because they have little faith in the system or do not believe that their votes will count. Perhaps with the recent memory of the disputed 2000 presidential election, Americans had reason to question whether every vote counts.

Election Day 2000 and Its Aftermath

On Election Day, November 7, 2000, Florida promised to be a key battleground in the presidential race between the Republican candidate, Governor George W. Bush of Texas, and the Democratic candidate, Vice President Al Gore. With its growing population, Florida would provide a significant number of votes in the Electoral College, a group of people chosen by the states to elect the president. Whoever won Florida would receive 25 electoral votes out of 538; only California, New York, and Texas had more electoral votes. Additionally, the race in Florida promised to be close; the Democrats and Republicans had split the last two presidential elections there.

On this important day, Roberta Tucker of Tallahassee was on her way to exercise her right to vote. What happened next to this African-American resident of the state capital attracted national attention. On the main road leading to a polling place in a heavily African-American voting district, a group of five Florida Highway Patrol (FHP) officers—all of them white—had set up a roadblock to stop passing cars. Though FHP officials later explained that the purpose of the roadblock was to check vehicles for faulty equipment, such as burned-out headlights, Tucker had a very different reaction. According to a report prepared by the U.S. Commission on Civil Rights:

> One of the troopers approached Ms. Tucker's car, asked for her driver's license, and after looking at it, returned it to her and allowed her to proceed. Ms. Tucker considered the trooper's actions to be "suspicious" because "nothing was checked, my lights, signals, or anything that [the police] usually check." ... She also recalled being "curious" about the checkpoint because she had never seen a checkpoint at this location. Ms. Tucker added that she felt "intimidated" because "it was an Election Day and it was a big election and there were only white officers there and like I said, they didn't ask me for anything else, so I was suspicious at that."[2]

The troopers had not received official permission to conduct this roadblock, and Florida's attorney general later acknowledged, "[A] checkpoint on that date, Election Day, was absolutely not necessary for law enforcement purposes."[3] Although the troopers' actions did not prevent Tucker from voting, the unauthorized roadblock signaled to many people another act in a long line of efforts to "disenfranchise" African Americans and other minorities—meaning to prevent them from voting.

Tucker's experience with the roadblock was largely overshadowed by widespread confusion and controversy throughout Florida during that fateful Election Day. In a nation in which voter turnout is already poor and faith in government is often weak, what happened in Florida that day led many Americans to completely lose faith in the electoral system and become convinced more than ever that their votes do not count. Countless Floridians were turned away from the polls because their registrations had been misplaced or their names had been misspelled on the voter rolls. Among those who did vote, malfunctioning punch card machines and confusing ballots left many Floridians wondering whether they had really voted for the candidate of their choice.

As Election Day 2000 ended across the country, the race was so close that the electoral votes in Florida would prove to provide the margin of victory for either Bush or Gore. Americans watched in confusion as news media outlets declared that Gore had won Florida's electoral votes but then changed their conclusion and declared Bush the winner. With both candidates claiming to have been the rightful victor, and after weeks of confusion, it would ultimately take the U.S. Supreme Court to settle the dispute, making George W. Bush the forty-third president of the United States.

On Election Night, the media had initially predicted that Gore had won in Florida because news sources base their predictions on "exit polls"—asking people leaving the polling stations which candidate they had selected. Generally, these polls are fairly accurate because people have no real reason to lie when asked. In Florida that night, however, the exit polls were misleading: Because of problems with some of the ballots used, many people either voted for the wrong candidate or did not vote for any candidate.

There is no standard method of voting in the United States. Some places use voting machines in which people pull a lever next to the name of the candidate of their choice. Other places use "bubble sheets," similar to those used for standardized tests. Many places in Florida used punch cards, which required voters to punch out a small piece of paper (or "chad") to vote for a candidate.

In Florida, local election officials determined the method of voting to be used in each polling place. Some of those choices proved to be extremely controversial, and—many Democrats believe—ultimately cost Gore the presidency. The most controversial ballot was the "butterfly ballot" used in Palm Beach County. Gore had expected to do well in the county, and exit

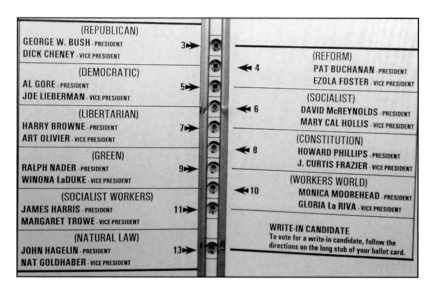

The layout of the infamous "butterfly ballot" used in some parts of Florida for the November 2000 presidential election may have led some confused voters to cast their votes for Reform Party candidate Pat Buchanan rather than Democratic Party candidate Al Gore.

polls confirmed his confidence. But as votes were tallied, Gore did much worse than expected, and Reform Party candidate Pat Buchanan made a surprisingly strong showing.

Why the unexpected results? Many blame the ballot itself. To vote for president using the butterfly ballot, the voter selected a circle out of a vertical column in the middle of the ballot. On either side of the column of circles, the candidates were listed, with arrows pointing to the corresponding circle. Many felt that the ballot was confusing, however. On the left-hand side of the page, the first candidate listed was Bush, and the second candidate listed was Gore. Voters for Bush needed only to select the first circle. Gore supporters, however, had to be alert enough to notice that Gore's circle was the *third* one down; on the right-hand side of the page, Pat Buchanan was listed at the top, and his arrow pointed to the second circle down. Anyone who selected the second circle thinking that he or she was voting for Gore was really voting for Buchanan.

As the media began to explain the theory that Buchanan's unexpected showing in Palm Beach County was due to the erroneous votes of Gore supporters, a number of people in the county who backed Gore clamored to have their votes corrected. Because the balloting was anonymous, however, there was no way to confirm whether people had voted "correctly" or "incorrectly." Even without that obstacle, an even more important question was how to distinguish whether someone had voted for Buchanan and then changed his or her mind.

Palm Beach was not the only county in Florida in which the ballots were called into question. Many voting precincts across the state used punch card ballots, which register votes when someone completely pushes out the chad next to the candidate's name. However—as people across the nation soon learned—voters sometimes do not completely push out the chad. In the weeks after the election, with both Gore and Bush claiming victory in Florida, the state began a recount of its ballots. Newspapers and television covered the recount extensively, as Americans learned about "hanging chads" and "dimpled chads."

Cooped up in rooms across Florida, groups of people examined punch card ballots; sometimes, the voter's choice was clear, but other times, the choice was not so clear. The recount teams were faced with trying to decide how to count hanging chads, which were detached at one or more corners but not completely punched out. Even more problematic was the dimpled chad (or "pregnant chad"), which bulged and appeared to have been pressed but was not detached from the ballot. The nation watched with anxious curiosity as news programs showed evaluators holding ballots up to the light or peering at them through magnifying glasses. Ultimately, in a controversial decision, the U.S. Supreme Court halted the recount, because there were no "specific standards" for determining the "intent of the voter."[4]

FROM THE BENCH

Bush v. Gore, No. 00-949 (Dec. 12, 2000)

Much of the controversy seems to revolve around ballot cards designed to be perforated by a stylus but which, either through error or deliberate omission, have not been perforated with sufficient precision for a machine to count them. In some cases a piece of the card—a chad—is hanging, say by two corners. In other cases there is no separation at all, just an indentation.

The Florida Supreme Court has ordered that the intent of the voter be discerned from such ballots. For purposes of resolving the equal protection challenge, it is not necessary to decide whether the Florida Supreme Court had the authority under the legislative scheme for resolving election disputes to define what a legal vote is and to mandate a manual recount implementing that definition. The recount mechanisms implemented in response to the decisions of the Florida Supreme Court do not satisfy the minimum requirement for non-arbitrary treatment of voters necessary to secure the fundamental right. Florida's basic command for the count of legally cast votes is to consider the "intent of the voter." . . . This is unobjectionable as an abstract proposition and a starting principle. The problem inheres in the absence of specific standards to ensure its equal application. . . .

The want of those rules here has led to unequal evaluation of ballots in various respects. . . . Should a county canvassing board count or not count a "dimpled chad" where the voter is able to successfully dislodge the chad in every other contest on that ballot? Here, the county canvassing boards disagree. . . . As seems to have been acknowledged at oral argument, the standards for accepting or rejecting contested ballots might vary not only from county to county but indeed within a single county from one recount team to another. . . .

Palm Beach County, for example, began the process with a 1990 guideline which precluded counting completely attached chads, switched to a rule that considered a vote to be legal if any light could be seen through a chad, changed back to the 1990 rule, and then abandoned any pretense of a per se rule, only to have a court order that the county consider dimpled chads legal. This is not a process with sufficient guarantees of equal treatment. . . .

The recount process, in its features here described, is inconsistent with the minimum procedures necessary to protect the fundamental right of each voter.

Does Every Vote Count?

Even though more than 100 million people voted in the 2000 presidential election, critics of the Supreme Court decision charged that the nine unelected members of the Court "elected" the president with a five-to-four vote. The reason that the events of Election Day 2000 were shocking to so many people is that voting is supposed to be the cornerstone of American democracy. The right to vote for almost everyone over the age of 18 secures the freedoms of what we believe to be the most open and democratic nation in the world. The presidential election had the potential to increase participation in democracy. Many people fail to vote, assuming that a single vote makes little difference. Yet, it was George W. Bush's slim margin of victory in Florida that decided the election. Had more Gore supporters voted—and many registered voters did not vote—Gore could have become president. The close election should have served as a lesson that every vote *does* count.

Instead, the lesson was wasted. Rather than thinking that their votes were important, many Floridians felt that their votes were useless. Many people, like journalist Neal Peirce, criticize America's "abysmal voter turnouts," which he reports are "138th in the world, sandwiched between Botswana and Chad"—two African nations.[5] The problem of low voter turnout is especially perplexing given how hard Americans have fought for the right to vote—a right once reserved for white male landowners. As a result of amendments to the U.S. Constitution, minority men won the right to vote in 1870, all women in 1920, and 18-year-olds in 1971. All of these amendments required dedicated and organized protest; yet today, voter participation often hovers around 50 percent.

In Minnesota, after the 2008 elections, quite a few people who thought their votes did not count were probably kicking themselves. In the race for U.S. senator, the incumbent, Republican Norm Coleman, faced a challenger whom many thought was a joke—former *Saturday Night Live* comedian Al

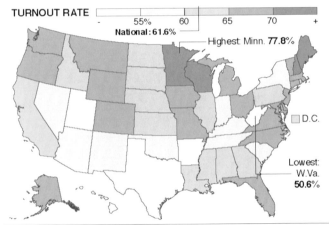

Minnesota led nation in voter turnout

At least 70 percent of Americans in Maine, New Hampshire, Wisconsin and Minnesota voted in the Nov. 4 election.

TURNOUT RATE

55% 60 65 70 +

National: 61.6%

Highest: Minn. **77.8%**

D.C.

Lowest: W.Va. **50.6%**

SOURCES: Associated Press; Prof. Michael McDonald, George Mason University   AP

In recent years, voter turnout has generally been low, even for national elections. During the 2008 presidential election, however, voter turnout was higher among Hispanic, black, and young voters. About 131 million citizens reported voting in the 2008 presidential election, an increase of 5 million from 2004.

Franken. The race was so close that the election results were not made official until the Minnesota Supreme Court ruled in June 2009 that Franken was the winner. Undoubtedly, a number of nonvoters on both sides wished that they had voted, whether to change the results of the election or to allow Franken to have taken his seat in the Senate sooner.

Why is voter turnout so low? Many people believe that our electoral system is badly damaged. Experiences like Roberta Tucker's remind us that some people still do not feel as if they can vote without fear. Yet, the news carries reports of dogs voting, dead people voting, even *dead dogs* voting. Giant corporations, such as the now-bankrupt energy company Enron, make headlines for widespread accounting fraud or other forms of wrongdoing, and the media reveal that these corporations have contributed enormous sums of money to elected officials for their reelection campaigns. This raises the question: Do corporations now "own" Congress? Perhaps people lose interest in voting after watching months of advertisements attacking the candidates—is *anyone* worth voting for?

Election Day 2000 served as a flashpoint for problems that have been smoldering for years. There has been a flurry of legislation since the 2000 election, at the federal level and in states around the nation. Few people, though, are satisfied. Some people think that further reforms are needed to ensure that every person has the right to have his or her vote counted.

Summary

Florida experienced widespread problems on Election Day 2000. Civil rights groups accused law enforcement of trying to prevent minorities from voting, and many people were turned away at the polls. Most significantly, thousands of ballots were called into question because outdated and ineffective punch cards did not indicate a clear choice for president. Without the questionable ballots, the election was too close to call. When it became clear that the close election in Florida would determine who would become the nation's next president, a statewide recount began, trying to interpret the questionable ballots. Ultimately, the Supreme Court decided 5-4 that the recount must stop, leading many to wonder who was controlling the election process—the American public or vested interests.

Voting Rights Require Strong Protections

For many civil rights activists, the events in Florida during the 2000 election were a warning sign that the voting rights of African Americans and other minorities were once again facing grave threats. Widespread disqualification of ballots signaled a reversal of more than three decades of progress in enforcing each citizen's right to vote. Laws are in a constant state of change, sometimes because circumstances change and sometimes because people find new ways of violating the laws. Throughout the history of federal voting rights legislation, there has constantly been a need to strengthen laws as people found new ways to violate the rights of others.

Although the Fifteenth Amendment to the U.S. Constitution, ratified in 1870, declared that citizens' right to vote could not be abridged based on race or color, blatant discrimination was alive and well nearly a century later throughout the South. Sometimes, the registrars refused to allow people to register. Other times, people used threats or other forms of retribution—such as employers firing African Americans who had registered to vote—to discourage minorities from registering and voting. Several civil rights organizations declared 1964 to be the "Freedom Summer" and sent armies of young civil rights workers to the South to help put an end to the discrimination.

These activists met with a chilly reception, facing the same threats and intimidation used to discourage minorities from voting. Gangs of thugs sometimes attacked the workers. The violence reached its peak on June 21, 1964, when three civil rights workers were murdered shortly after being released from jail; they had been arrested on questionable charges while investigating the burning of a church.

In its inquiry, the Federal Bureau of Investigation (FBI) uncovered a plot that involved local law enforcement and the Ku Klux Klan in Mississippi, but it also brought to light the many indignities that African Americans faced on a daily basis. During the investigation, agents discovered "additional civil rights violations other than the three murder victims," concluding: "[T]here appeared to be a conspiracy on the part of the prime suspects; namely, the Sheriff, his Deputy, and others who are closely associated with the Sheriff's Office . . . to deprive the colored population of their civil rights."[1]

The murders of the three young men brought national attention to voting rights and spurred Congress to act. In 1965, Congress enacted the Voting Rights Act,[2] which prohibited states from using written tests, "moral character" standards, or "poll taxes"—payments required in order to vote—as ways of excluding otherwise eligible voters. Congress had found that some states used such tactics to reduce the number of minority voters. The act also prohibited anyone—state official or not—from using "intimidation, threats, or coercion" to prevent people from voting. The law did not, however, prohibit the bureaucracy, or "red tape," that in many states made registering to vote difficult for everyone.

The National Voter Registration Act of 1993,[3] commonly called the "Motor Voter" law, required states to make registering to vote much easier by increasing the number of places at which people could register. The law earned its nickname by requiring that states allow people to register to vote when they receive or renew a driver's license. The law also requires states to provide voter registration at public assistance ("welfare") offices, as well as many other state government offices, such as those issuing hunting and fishing licenses.

In the aftermath of the disputed 2000 presidential election, Congress passed the Help America Vote Act[4] in 2002. In response to criticisms of voters being turned away from the polls, the law requires states to implement "provisional balloting," a system in which people whose registration status cannot be verified are allowed to cast a provisional ballot, which is kept separate from other ballots. If the voter's registration status can later be verified, then the vote will count; the system therefore will cause some delay in determining the outcome of close races as election officials verify the status of any provisional ballots collected.

Despite the passage of these acts, many people still feel that the laws on the books do not do enough to protect the rights of every eligible adult citizen to vote. They fear that many people will continue to have their efforts to register rebuffed, to be turned away at the polls, or to have their ballots discarded. Despite the many state and federal laws designed to protect voting rights, many people believe that systematic efforts to disenfranchise minorities, immigrants, and other targeted groups continue. Critics charge that the laws are either ignored or are manipulated as the "powers that be" find new ways to skirt the laws.

Barriers to voting disproportionately affect immigrants, minorities, and the poor.

Over the years, disenfranchisement of minorities has taken many forms. Since the ratification of the Fifteenth Amendment

THE LETTER OF THE LAW

Help America Vote Act, § 303

(a) Computerized Statewide Voter Registration List Requirements.— . . .

    (5) Verification of voter registration information.—

        (A) Requiring provision of certain information by applicants.—

            (i) In general.—Except as provided in clause (ii), notwithstanding any other provision of law, an application for voter registration for an election for Federal office may not be accepted or processed by a State unless the application includes—

                (I) in the case of an applicant who has been issued a current and valid driver's license, the applicant's driver's license number; or

                (II) in the case of any other applicant (other than an applicant to whom clause (ii) applies), the last 4 digits of the applicant's social security number.

            (ii) Special rule for applicants without driver's license or social security number.—If an applicant for voter registration for an election for Federal office has not been issued a current and valid driver's license or a social security number, the State shall assign the applicant a number which will serve to identify the applicant for voter registration purposes. . . .

            (iii) Determination of validity of numbers provided.—The State shall determine whether the information provided by an individual is sufficient to meet the requirements of this subparagraph, in accordance with State law. . . .

(b) Requirements for Voters Who Register by Mail.—

    (1) In general.— . . . [A] State shall, in a uniform and nondiscriminatory manner, require an individual to meet the requirements of paragraph (2) if—

        (A) the individual registered to vote in a jurisdiction by mail; and in 1870, it had been illegal for states to deny people the right to vote based on their race. The events leading up to the passage of the Voting Rights Act, however, had made it clear that state officials and private citizens were determined to keep minorities

---

(B)(i) the individual has not previously voted in an election for Federal office in the State; or

(ii) the individual has not previously voted in such an election in the jurisdiction and the jurisdiction is located in a State that does not have a computerized list that complies with the requirements of subsection (a).

(2) Requirements.—

(A) In general.—An individual meets the requirements of this paragraph if the individual—

(i) in the case of an individual who votes in person—(I) presents to the appropriate State or local election official a current and valid photo identification; or

(II) presents to the appropriate State or local election official a copy of a current utility bill, bank statement, government check, paycheck, or other government document that shows the name and address of the voter. . . .

(B) Fail-safe voting.—

(i) In person.—An individual who desires to vote in person, but who does not meet the requirements of subparagraph (A)(i), may cast a provisional ballot under section 302(a). . . .

(4) Contents of mail-in registration form.—

(A) In general.—The mail voter registration form ... shall include the following:

(i) The question "Are you a citizen of the United States of America?" and boxes for the applicant to check to indicate whether the applicant is or is not a citizen of the United States.

Source: Help America Vote Act, 42 U.S.C. § 15483.

from voting. While today, outright discrimination is illegal, many civil rights groups have shifted their focus on barriers to registration and voting, many of which disproportionately affect immigrants, minorities, and the poor.

It is likely that some problems on Election Day are unavoidable. Most people staffing the polls are not full-time election workers; rather, they are hired for the day to work at the polls. People are supposed to vote in a designated precinct, which can change when people move, even if they move a short distance. Purchasing new voting equipment is usually not a priority for states or counties, which have many other financial obligations. When filling out ballots, some human error is unavoidable, and it is likely that errors will also occur when tabulating millions of votes.

It is likely human error rather than deliberate misconduct that leads to both the denial of voting rights and the casting of ballots by ineligible voters. A 2007 exposé by the *New York Times* revealed, "Mistakes and lapses in enforcing voting and registration rules routinely occur in elections, allowing thousands of ineligible voters to go to the polls. But the federal cases provide little evidence of widespread, organized fraud."[5]

While 100 percent voting accuracy might not be achievable, many people think that the states can do a better job each Election Day. Furthermore, many would like to see improvements made so that every voting precinct—whether it is in a wealthy suburb, an inner-city neighborhood, or a poor rural county—is on equal footing. When it comes to errors that lead to votes not being counted, minorities and the poor often seem to bear the brunt of the problem. In its review of the 2000 election in Florida, the U.S Commission on Civil Rights concluded: "African Americans . . . were nearly 10 times more likely than white voters to have their ballots rejected in the November 2000 election."[6] The commission attributed the disproportionate effect on minorities to the use of outdated equipment—such as punch card machines—in counties with large minority populations:

For example, in Gadsden County, the only county in the state with an African American majority, approximately one in eight voters was disenfranchised. In Leon County, on the other hand, which is home to the prosperous state capital and two state universities, fewer than two votes in 1,000 were not counted. In Florida, of the 100 precincts with the highest numbers of disqualified ballots, 83 of them are majority-black precincts.[7]

Such problems were not unique to Florida. Noting at a congressional hearing that, in her home state of Georgia, African-American voters were more likely to be required to use outdated and inefficient punch card machines, which are more likely to invalidate votes, former U.S. Representative Cynthia McKinney testified: "In the majority-black precincts of my district, the chaos was so pervasive it could have been planned. . . . There were poorly trained elections workers, old equipment, and overcrowded precincts. . . . [Voters had] to stand in line, sometimes outside in the rain and sometimes for as many as five hours."[8]

Many groups are concerned that, although immigrants who become citizens are legally entitled to vote, barriers such as identification requirements and English-only ballots discourage them from voting. In a 2008 case in which the majority of the U.S. Supreme Court upheld Indiana's law requiring a driver's license or state-issued photo identification card to vote, Justice David Souter dissented, pointing out the law's unfairness to certain groups. He noted:

> The need to travel to a [bureau of motor vehicles] branch will affect voters according to their circumstances, with the average person probably viewing it as nothing more than an inconvenience. Poor, old, and disabled voters who do not drive a car, however, may find the trip prohibitive.[9]

Current voting rights laws are not enforced strongly enough.

Many civil rights advocates believe that incidents of continued disenfranchisement of the poor, minorities, and immigrants provide proof that our nation's voting rights laws need to be strengthened. As Representative McKinney noted, the Voting Rights Act is subject to abuse by people who obey the letter of the law but violate the spirit of the law. Reflecting on the confusion that occurred in her district during the 2000 election, she charged:

> [P]erhaps the [county] leaders ... don't want large voter participation from the black residents on its south side. That's the only way I can explain the failure to adequately fund the elections office for the past four years. I would argue that this is a subtle violation of the Voting Rights Act with the intent and effect of suppressing the minority vote.[10]

Many civil rights supporters fear that more recent laws, such as the Motor Voter law and the Help America Vote Act, will also be subject to manipulation. Though the Motor Voter law—with its provision that driver's license and welfare offices must actively offer voter registration opportunities—was highly touted as a way to register large numbers of poor and minority voters, the implementation of the law has been far from perfect.

In fact, one key provision of the Voting Rights Act has come under attack. The federal law requires states, counties, and localities to obtain "preclearance" from the federal government before changing their election procedures. "Political subdivisions" can seek a "bailout" from these requirements if they have a strong track record of fair elections, however. A utility district, which elects a board to regulate public utilities such as electricity, located in Texas challenged the constitutionality of the preclearance requirements. A number of conservative groups joined the utility district's cause in a lawsuit. In the case, *Northwest Austin Municipal Utility District No. 1 v. Holder,* the Legal Defense and Educational

Minorities in the United States, particularly women and African Americans, struggled for many years to win the right to vote. In March 1965, Martin Luther King Jr. *(center, in black overcoat)* led a group of civil rights activists to the Alabama state capital in a demonstration to encourage voter registration.

Fund of the National Association for the Advancement of Colored People (NAACP) submitted a brief to the Supreme Court, arguing that the preclearance requirements should be maintained:

> Despite unquestionable progress since 1965, voting discrimination in covered jurisdictions has proven a persistent threat to the rights guaranteed by the Fourteenth and Fifteenth Amendments.... Gains in minority registration often lead to the use of sophisticated forms of purposeful discrimination designed to cancel out minority voting strength.[11]

Additionally, the NAACP's Legal Defense and Educational Fund answered arguments that efforts to suppress the vote were the acts of rogue local officials acting contrary to the law: "Many incidents of discrimination that appear localized actually involve intentionally discriminatory actions taken by both local officials and the State."[12]

As the Legal Defense and Educational Fund noted, the increasing number of Hispanic voters in Texas made them particularly at risk of voter suppression: "Minority voters are often the most likely to face discrimination when they are gaining numerical strength and on the verge of exercising newfound political power."[13] The brief cited numerous incidents in which the federal government had rejected changes proposed by Texas or its counties, including efforts to limit the number of congressional districts in which Hispanic voters would make up the majority and efforts to keep students at a historically black university from voting in county elections.

The case in Texas is not the only one that has worried advocates of voting rights. The U.S. Commission on Civil Rights has found serious flaws in Florida's voter registration process. For example, people who moved to other counties were issued new driver's licenses, but the department of motor vehicles did not forward their voter registrations to their new counties of residence. Additionally, the department of motor vehicles was unable to account for many voter registrations. The commission's report cited the example of one married couple who had registered to vote when they obtained their driver's licenses. Although the

THE LETTER OF THE LAW

The "Motor Voter" Law's Registration Requirements

[E]ach State shall establish procedures to register to vote in elections for Federal office …

(1) Each State motor vehicle driver's license application (including any renewal application) submitted to the appropriate State motor vehicle authority under State law shall serve as an application for voter registration with respect to elections for Federal office unless the applicant fails to sign the voter registration application.

(2) An application for voter registration submitted under paragraph (1) shall be considered as updating any previous voter registration by the applicant.…

(1) Each State shall designate agencies for the registration of voters in elections for Federal office.

(2) Each State shall designate as voter registration agencies—

   (A) all offices in the State that provide public assistance; and

   (B) all offices in the State that provide State-funded programs primarily engaged in providing services to persons with disabilities.

(3) (A) In addition to voter registration agencies designated under paragraph (2), each State shall designate other offices within the State as voter registration agencies.

   (B) Voter registration agencies designated under subparagraph (A) may include—

      (i) State or local government offices such as public libraries, public schools, offices of city and county clerks (including marriage license bureaus), fishing and hunting license bureaus, government revenue offices, unemployment compensation offices, and offices not described in paragraph (2)(B) that provide services to persons with disabilities; and

      (ii) Federal and nongovernmental offices, with the agreement of such offices.

Source: National Voter Registration Act, 42 U.S.C. §§ 1973gg-2-1973gg-5.

department's records indicated that the couple had indeed registered to vote, the county election office did not have copies of these registrations. The commission concluded: "Mr. and Mrs. Seamans properly registered to vote at their driver license office and were deprived of their right to vote on Election Day."[14]

The Help America Vote Act does not do enough to protect voters' rights.

Although the Help America Vote Act was passed in 2002 as an effort to remedy such mistakes, many people think that the law does not do enough to correct the inequities of the current system. For example, the identification requirements have generated criticism. Senator Charles Schumer, a Democrat from New York who voted against the law, argued that the identification requirements would send the wrong message to voters who have emigrated from countries with oppressive regimes:

> [T]hink of the new immigrant who waited five years and has just become a voter, who doesn't have a car, who is just learning English, and who is afraid of the government where that immigrant came from. You say, *You have to do this, this, this, and this. . . .*
>
> I have seen the look on the faces of first-time voters who waited in line with their eyes bright with the first chance to exercise their franchise and then were turned away. And they never come back again.[15]

In theory, the provisional balloting system seems to guarantee people that their vote will be counted, but many people are not so sure that it will have that effect in practice. The process of verifying the registrations of people casting provisional ballots is subject to the same errors as verifying registrations on site. The National Council of La Raza, a Hispanic civil rights and advocacy group, opposed the legislation, criticizing what it called "an intrusive, error-prone requirement that voters provide a driver's license number or, in the event they do not have one, the last four digits of their Social Security number." According to the group, this verification process could lead to disenfranchisement: "Election officials must independently verify the number before registering someone, and any individual who has either number but fails to provide it will not be registered."[16] Other groups, such as the American Civil Liberties Union (ACLU), expressed similar concerns.

Summary

Though prohibited by the U.S. Constitution, there is a long history of voter discrimination against minorities, immigrants, and the poor. Each time the government has passed a law, new types of discrimination have surfaced; today, civil rights activists believe that discrimination is subtler but still exists. The latest effort to prevent disenfranchisement is the Help America Vote Act of 2002, but many doubt that it does enough to halt disenfranchisement of minorities, immigrants, and the poor.

Strict Registration Requirements Prevent Fraud

Despite anecdotal evidence that eligible voters have been denied the right to vote, not everybody is convinced that stronger voting rights laws are the answer. Many people, especially politically conservative Republicans, feel that voting rights laws go too far. They feel that fault for people being turned away from the polls lies not with the system but with the individual voters who did not ensure that they were properly registered. Of greater concern, they believe, is that the generous protections afforded by federal laws actually encourage voter fraud.

Countering arguments that people are too frequently turned away from the polls, critics of generous voting rights laws often use the example of how little trouble Mabel and Holly Briscoe had registering to vote in Maryland. Despite claims that older people and people who have just reached voting age are often denied the right to vote, Mabel and Holly had no problems registering at a driver's license office in Maryland, even though Mabel was in her eighties and Holly was 18.

It took Maryland officials two years to notice that anything was wrong with Holly's registration form. Eventually, however, they figured out the problem: Holly was 18 only when her age was measured in *dog years*. State officials discovered the problem when they called Holly for jury duty and Mabel was forced to admit that she had falsified her pet terrier's registration form to prove just how easy the Motor Voter law made voter fraud.

Mabel had not intended for anyone to vote in Holly's name; rather she registered her dog to vote as a "personal experiment in civil disobedience."[1] She was trying to prove that the Motor Voter law made it too easy for people (not to mention dogs) to vote. Though Maryland officials tried to prosecute her for voter fraud, they ended up dropping the charges in exchange for community service.

Many people are convinced that the most important weakness of today's electoral system is not that people are being denied the right to register and vote. They believe that each person has a responsibility to register and vote, and "voting rights" laws merely encourage apathetic voters. Many Republicans have accused the Democratic Party of making "voting rights" an issue not out of fairness, but in an effort to increase the number of Democratic voters. The result, they charge, is a system riddled with fraud. Though the Help America Vote Act of 2002 contains antifraud provisions, some Republican politicians are concerned that states will not strictly enforce the provisions.

Special efforts to register immigrants, minorities, and the poor are politically motivated.

Although supporters of voting rights laws frequently speak of the need to protect the rights of immigrants, minorities, and the poor as a matter of civil rights, many Republicans counter that such laws simply represent partisan efforts by Democrats to register people who have traditionally voted

Democratic. When the Motor Voter law was passed during the Clinton administration, Republicans widely criticized the law as a thinly veiled effort by the Democratic Party to woo voters who supported its social welfare programs. Especially troubling to many critics was the provision requiring that welfare offices provide voter-registration forms: The Republican Party favored sweeping welfare reform, making it less likely that welfare recipients would vote Republican.

Many conservative critics have suggested that voting rights laws do not remove barriers to voting as much as they try to encourage voting among people who are unwilling to make any special efforts to register to vote. Jonah Goldberg, editor of the online edition of the *National Review*, wrote: "Motor-voter supporters, and others who bemoan low turnout, have never satisfactorily addressed a fundamental question: Why should we care that people who don't care enough to vote aren't voting?"[2] In their opinion, voting is a privilege as well as a right, and therefore people can be expected to make special efforts to register and vote. Conservatives have poked fun at endeavors such as "Rock the Vote," in which popular musicians encourage young people to register and vote.

Before the 2008 presidential election, conservative columnist Michelle Malkin complained that the Association of Community Organizations for Reform Now (ACORN), for whom Barack Obama had once worked, was engaging in blatantly partisan efforts to register people to vote for Obama. Because the group received a significant portion of its funds from the federal government, it was required to engage only in nonpartisan activity (not favoring any candidate or party). "It's an all-out scramble to scrape up every last unregistered voter sympathetic to Obama's big-government vision," she wrote.[3]

Another example of a voter-registration drive that drew heavy criticism was the effort to register Native American voters during the 2002 senatorial election in South Dakota. The combined efforts of the state and national Democratic parties led to the registration of 17,000 new voters in the sparsely populated state. Although it was true that, before the registration campaign, many Native Americans living on the state's nine reservations had either not registered to vote or had registered but not regularly voted, some criticized the Democratic Party's efforts as designed to win votes rather than to encourage civic participation. Ultimately, in the statewide senatorial election, the Democratic candidate, Tim Johnson, beat his Republican challenger by 524 votes.

In an article for the *National Review*, Byron York criticized the Democrats' tactics for registering voters, calling their practice of paying "bounty hunters" $3 for each person they registered to vote an "invitation to fraud."[4] He also questioned the Democrats' Election Day activities, including renting vans and hiring drivers to bring people to the polls. Republican poll volunteer Ed Assman told York that Democratic poll workers were giving cash to the van drivers. "I heard the driver say, 'We need money.' . . . The guy rolled out cash and gave cash to each guy," Assman said.[5] Although the Democrats explained that this was "gas money," and the state's attorney general found no credible evidence of paying people to vote, news of drivers being given cash raised many suspicions.

In efforts to register immigrants, who have traditionally voted overwhelmingly Democratic, some Republicans have suggested that Democrats have even targeted noncitizens. Jim Boulet Jr., executive director of English First, an organization supporting adoption of English as the United States' official language, criticized the Democratic Party for sending a letter, in English and Spanish, to people not registered to vote encouraging them to register; the letter reached at least one noncitizen and probably many others. Boulet also asserted that, during the administration of Democrat Bill Clinton, immigration laws were bent or broken in an effort to register more immigrant voters. He writes: "Al Gore helped Bill Clinton trade permanent U.S. citizenship for Democratic votes in 1996 and beyond," charging the former vice president with turning Citizenship USA, a program designed to help immigrants become citizens, "into 'a pro-Democrat voter mill' in which English tests were waived and criminal records of prospective citizens were swept under the rug."[6]

Voter abuses have been overstated to increase the political power of the Democratic Party.

Many critics also charge that claims of disenfranchisement are not genuinely motivated by concern that voters need to have their voices heard but are really partisan efforts by the Democratic Party to increase votes for their candidates. Although the U.S. Commission on Civil Rights concluded that widespread voter disenfranchisement occurred in Florida during the 2000 presidential election, many have disputed that claim, believing instead that attempts to discredit the Florida election constituted a partisan effort by Democrats to weaken public confidence in the incoming president, George W. Bush.

In fact, two members of the commission filed a dissenting report criticizing the commission's findings. Commissioners Abigail Thernstrom and Russell G. Redenbaugh wrote that the number of disqualified ballots was not evidence of disenfranchisement: "Disenfranchisement is not the same thing as voter error. [Many of the disqualified ballots] are due to voter error. Or machine error, which is random, and thus cannot 'disenfranchise' any population group."[7] The dissenting commissioners added that, in addition to being unsupported by the facts, accusations of disenfranchisement were being levied at the wrong people. Although much of the criticism focused on Governor Jeb Bush (President Bush's brother), and Secretary of State Katherine Harris, also a Republican, the supervision of elections was done on the county level. The commissioners noted: "Of the 25 Florida counties with the highest rate of vote spoilage . . . [a]ll but one . . . had Democratic chief election officers, and the one exception was in the hands of an official with no party affiliation."[8] In other words, local Democratic politicians had botched the election, but after Bush won the presidential race, Democrats used charges of racism and partisanship to criticize Florida's Republican administration and call the election into doubt.

Conservative groups have continued to raise questions about the ongoing need for federal voting rights laws, portraying election misconduct as largely a thing of the past. In a 2009 U.S. Supreme Court case, the conservative Pacific Legal Foundation argued that certain aspects of the Voting Rights Act should be held unconstitutional:

> Changes in the social and political landscape do not justify the application of [the Voting Rights Act's] measures to the same jurisdictions for twenty-five more years. Today, even in the South, political and social conditions are far different from what they were forty years ago when certain state legislatures and county officials did whatever was necessary to ensure the continued disenfranchisement of black voters. Government action approaching such blatantly racist conduct could not even exist today given this country's growing shift to a color-blind society that just recently saw the election of our nation's first black President, the increasing intolerance for racism among most Americans, and the ever present scrutiny of news media.[9]

So-called voting rights laws have caused widespread fraud.

The story of Mabel Briscoe, who registered her dog to vote in Maryland, attracted national headlines, mostly as a humorous anecdote. The terrier never voted, and so no harm was done, many thought. Yet, like the Maryland officials who wanted to prosecute the 82-year-old woman, some people did not think that the story was funny at all. Rather, the story was a reminder that some people not only register their dogs to vote, but they take advantage of the registrations to vote illegally.

As Malkin noted in her criticism of ACORN's voter-registration efforts, which she alleged were clearly in support of Barack Obama's candidacy, numerous allegations of fraud had

FROM THE BENCH

Northwest Austin Municipal Utility District No. 1 v. Holder, No. 08-322 (June 22, 2009)

In a 2009 case, the U.S. Supreme Court ruled that a utility district in Texas could petition for a "bailout" from certain requirements of the Voting Rights Act. In general, states, counties, and other "political subdivisions" are required to gain "preclearance" from the federal government before changing their election procedures. The federal government must confirm that the proposed changes will not deny any group the right to vote. A utility district in Travis County, Texas, which held elections for its utility board members (people who approve raising electricity prices, for example), argued that it should be "bailed out" because the utility district had no history of voter discrimination. One of the utility district's arguments was that the law was unconstitutional.

The Supreme Court decided the case by interpreting the law in the utility district's favor and therefore did not have to decide the difficult question of whether the law was constitutional. Writing for the majority, however, Chief Justice John Roberts expressed his doubts. His opinion suggests that changes in the nation's racial climate lessen the need for the federal government to scrutinize the election practices of cities, counties, and states. He wrote:

> More than 40 years ago, this Court concluded that "exceptional conditions" prevailing in certain parts of the country justified extraordinary [voting rights] legislation otherwise unfamiliar to our federal system. . . . In part due to the success of that legislation, we are now a very different Nation. Whether conditions continue to justify such legislation is a difficult constitutional question we do not answer today. We conclude instead that the Voting Rights Act permits all political subdivisions, including the district in this case, to seek relief from its preclearance requirements.

emerged. Among the allegations were ACORN workers submitting multiple registrations for voters, forging signatures of
names taken from phone books, and submitting phony registrations in the names of former Dallas Cowboys football players.
"Quantity over quality. That's the ACORN way—and the fraud
allegations keep piling up," she wrote.[10]

Senator Christopher ("Kit") Bond, a Missouri Republican,
alleged that illegal voting was rampant in his state—including
at least one case of a *dead dog* that had supposedly cast a ballot.
According to Bond: "3,000 ballots [were] dropped off before the
mayoral primary in St. Louis in 2001.... [M]ost of those 3,000
were in the same handwriting and were for new registrants on
one or two city blocks."[11]

John Samples, the director of the Center for Representative
Government at the Cato Institute, attributed the widespread
voting fraud to efforts by political parties to register minority
voters. Referring to the same St. Louis mayoral election criticized
by Bond, Samples testified before a Senate committee:

> [A] national campaign—promoted by Democrats—to
> register more African-American voters and get them
> to the polling booth ... delivered 3,800 voter registra-
> tion cards [on] the deadline for the March mayoral
> primary. ...
>
> [N]early all of [the cards] were fraudulent. Many
> of them sought to register prominent people, dead or
> alive—as well as at least three deceased aldermen and a
> dog. ... They also found cards for convicted felons and
> for residents who did not seek to register themselves in
> the primary.[12]

Samples also testified that such problems were by no means
limited to Missouri and identified other states in which the
Motor Voter law had led to voter fraud:

In Indiana ... tens of thousands of people appear on the voter rolls more than once ... more than 300 dead people were registered, and ... three convicted killers and two convicted child molesters were on the rolls. In general, experts believe one in five names on the rolls in Indiana do not belong there. A recent study in Georgia found more than 15,000 dead people on active voting rolls statewide. Alaska, according to Federal Election Commission, had 502,968 names on its voter rolls in 1998. The census estimates only 437,000 people of voting age were living in the state that year.[13]

Samples asserted that the Motor Voter law had made it impossible for states to control voter fraud. At the same time that the law made it much easier for people to submit fraudulent registrations, it also made it much more difficult for states to remove people from the list of registered voters:

[To] remove a voter who has moved from the rolls of a voting district, the local jurisdiction has two choices. First, they could get written confirmation of the move from the citizen. Lacking that, the jurisdiction had to send a notice to the voter. If the notice card was not returned and the person did not vote in two general elections for Federal office after the notice was sent, then the jurisdiction could remove their name from the rolls.[14]

Strict enforcement of the Help America Vote Act is necessary to prevent future fraud.

While Congress deliberated the Help America Vote Act, much of the controversy centered on the law's antifraud provisions, with the split following strict party lines. The reason that Congress took nearly two years to respond to the widespread problems of the 2000 election with this law streamlining registration and voting procedures was that Democrats viewed strict antifraud provisions as a way to disenfranchise voters, while Republicans thought that any law making it easier for eligible citizens to register and vote must simultaneously make it more difficult for dishonest people to fraudulently register and vote.

During Senate debates, Senator Bond expressed frustration with Democratic opposition to provisions requiring that first-time voters who register by mail provide a form of identification to vote: "[We] devised a compromise that ... did not impose any unreasonable restrictions on voters who might not have a driver's license, for example. That is why we said voters can use a bank statement, a government check, utility bill, anything that has your name and address on it."[15]

THE LETTER OF THE LAW

The "Motor Voter" Law's List Maintenance Requirements

(d) Removal of names from voting rolls

    (1) A State shall not remove the name of a registrant from the official list of eligible voters in elections for Federal office on the ground that the registrant has changed residence unless the registrant—

    (A) confirms in writing that the registrant has changed residence to a place outside the registrar's jurisdiction in which the registrant is registered; or

    (B) (i) has failed to respond to a notice described in paragraph (2); and

    (ii) has not voted or appeared to vote (and, if necessary, correct the registrar's record of the registrant's address) in an election during the period beginning on the date of the notice and ending on the day after the date of the second general election for Federal office that occurs after the date of the notice.

    (2) A notice is described in this paragraph if it is a postage prepaid and pre-addressed return card, sent by forwardable mail, on which the registrant may state his or her current address. . . .

Source: National Voter Registration Act, 42 U.S.C. § 1973gg.

Unable to defeat the law's identification requirements, Democrats waged a battle in the press after passage of the law, arguing that states could make up their own minds about allowing people to register. Senator Christopher Dodd, a Connecticut Democrat, told the *New York Times*, "The legislation does not establish federal registration eligibility requirements. . . . Nothing in this legislation prohibits a state from registering an applicant once the verification process takes place," which, according to the article, includes cases in which "a would-be voter provides inaccurate or incomplete information."[16]

Senator Bond challenged his colleague's interpretation of the law: "It is the intent of Congress to impose a new federal mandate for voter registration."[17] Democrats and civil rights organizations might pressure states to continue processing inaccurate or incomplete applications—for example, applications in which the registrant fails to answer the question, "Are you a citizen of the United States of America?" Dodd has suggested that the legislation requires the states to ask the question but does not require them to invalidate applications in which the answer is left blank. But Republicans like Bond believe that, unless states follow the spirit of the law and only register voters who provide complete, accurate information, rampant voter fraud will continue.

Summary

Many political conservatives believe that the biggest problem facing American elections is not that people are being denied the right to vote but that too many people are voting fraudulently. They support stricter registration and identification requirements and question massive voter-registration drives. They believe that each person should take responsibility to register and vote. Many Republicans, believing that many "voting rights" measures are in fact disguised efforts to gain Democratic votes, want to see voting fraud measures strictly enforced.

Money Corrupts American Democracy

Running successfully for a prominent political office in the United States requires an incredible amount of money. According to Kathleen Murphy, who covers election issues for Stateline.org, the *losing* candidate in the 2002 governor's race in Texas spent close to $70 million, while "[c]andidates for governor in New York could have bought every voter two Big Macs with fries and Cokes for about half the amount they spent on the race."[1] Considering that nearly 12 million registered voters live in the state, that's a lot of hamburgers!

Most money for campaigns has come from contributions from individuals, corporations, unions, or special-interest groups. Some politicians are concerned that the amount of money being pumped into political campaigns has created a corrupt government, in which elected officials care more about contributors than they do about the people who elect them.

Champions of "campaign finance reform" such as Senators John McCain and Russ Feingold believe that limits on fund-raising activities are needed to preserve the integrity of American democracy. Although McCain and Feingold won passage of a federal law, the Bipartisan Campaign Reform Act of 2002 (BCRA), the U.S. Supreme Court overturned provisions of that law in *Citizens United v. Federal Election Commission* (2010). It is therefore likely that the campaign finance debate will continue in the courts and in Congress for years to come.

Some of the most controversial provisions of federal election laws deal with campaign contributions, including:

- Limits on individual campaign contributions of $2,000 per candidate (raised by BCRA from the previous limit of $1,000).[2]
- Prohibition of most campaign contributions by corporations and labor unions (extended by BCRA to ban contributions to political parties).[3]

Before passage of BCRA, federal election law was largely a result of decisions by the Federal Election Commission (a federal agency) and the landmark 1976 Supreme Court decision in *Buckley v. Valeo*. In that case, the Court upheld limits on contributions to candidates; however, the Court noted that the First Amendment's guarantee of free speech invalidated many other aspects of federal election law.

Although federal law limited their ability to contribute money directly to candidates, many corporations, labor unions, and wealthy individuals still wanted to influence the political process. As a result, they began to make large contributions to the Democratic and Republican parties. Although the contributions allowed the parties to campaign for candidates, the contributions did not technically violate the law, earning such contributions the nickname "soft money." Senator Feingold wrote that soft money transforms "our representative democracy" into a "corporate democracy, in which

From left, Representative Christopher Shays (R-Conn.), Representative
Martin T. Meehan (D-Mass.), Senator Russell D. Feingold (D-Wis.), Senator
James M. Jeffords (I-Vt.), and Senator John McCain (R-Ariz.) discuss the
Bipartisan Campaign Reform Act of 2002, also known as the McCain–
Feingold Act, at a news conference. These politicians have led the
campaign-reform effort in recent years.

the 'one person, one vote' principle is supplanted by a system
that allocates influence over the political process in proportion
to the amount of money an individual or group puts into that
process."[4]

Although BCRA banned soft money, there have been numerous court challenges to the law, and campaign finance reformers
have found themselves having to continue to defend the ban on
soft money. Reformers firmly believe that soft money has a corrupting influence on Congress and has caused the public to lose
faith in the political process. They reject the idea that campaign
contributions are a form of "free speech" protected by the First

Amendment, believing that if anything, political contributions take power away from individual voters and concentrate it in the hands of the wealthy.

Soft money obligates elected officials to corporate interests rather than the public interest. The movement for campaign finance reform gained momentum as a growing number of people began to believe that many members of Congress no longer represented the interests of the people who elected them. Instead, it was feared that members of Congress primarily represented the interests of the corporations and other interest groups making the soft-money donations that allowed them to campaign successfully.

Supporters of campaign finance reform do not necessarily accuse members of Congress and other politicians of allowing their votes to be bought; however, the line between accepting a bribe and being overly influenced by campaign contributions can be somewhat murky. To give an illustration, environmental laws can have an enormous impact on the profitability of chemical manufacturers. If, while Congress was debating new

THE LETTER OF THE LAW

Bipartisan Campaign Reform Act Subjects "Soft Money" to Same Limits as Other Contributions

SOFT MONEY OF POLITICAL PARTIES.

(a) NATIONAL COMMITTEES.—

(1) IN GENERAL.—A national committee of a political party (including a national congressional campaign committee of a political party) may not solicit, receive, or direct to another person a contribution, donation, or transfer of funds or any other thing of value, or spend any funds, that are not subject to the limitations, prohibitions, and reporting requirements of this Act.

Source: Bipartisan Campaign Reform Act, 42 U.S.C., sec. 441i.

pollution laws, a chemical company trying to influence a particular senator's vote gave him or her $50,000 to buy a new car, this payment would constitute bribery, a serious crime. Yet, if the same chemical company gave $50,000 to the senator's political party to help with a reelection campaign, this type of soft-money contribution would have been perfectly legal before passage of the BCRA.

Although the soft-money contribution in this illustration would not have obliged the senator to support the chemical company's position, the desire for future financial support would be likely to have a tremendous influence on his or her vote. Supporters of campaign finance reform view this influence as a problem in itself. Senator Christopher Dodd has argued:

> Money ... threatens to drown out the voice of the average voter of average means; money ... creates the appearance that a wealthy few have a disproportionate say over public policy; and money ... places extensive demands on the time of candidates—time that they and the voters believe is better spent discussing and debating the issues of the day.[5]

Surprisingly, despite the possibility of gaining political influence through soft-money contributions, not all business leaders opposed BCRA's soft-money ban. Denouncing what it called the "perversion of the soft-money system into a widely acknowledged 'pay to play' scheme by both major parties,"[6] the Committee for Economic Development, a group of business leaders and educators, argued that the soft-money system placed unfair pressures on businesses: "Because the stakes are so high for solicited businesses, the reality is that soft-money payments ... are commonly made out of fear of the consequences of refusing to give or refusing to give enough."[7]

The effect of corporate campaign spending has not escaped public notice. Companies such as Enron, the energy company that made headlines through widespread accounting irregularities, and Phillip Morris, which profited from selling hazardous tobacco products, were significant soft-money donors. These companies curried favor in Congress while members of the public lost their retirement savings because of the drop in Enron's stock price or suffered or died from the harmful effects of smoking. The influence of such corporations with elected officials has eroded the public's confidence in American democracy.

Arguing in support of BCRA in a 2001 Senate debate, Senator McCain said: "[According to] a poll that *Time* magazine has conducted over many years ... [in] 1961, 76 percent of Americans said yes to the question, 'Do you trust your government to do the right thing?' This year, only 19 percent of Americans still believe that."[8] And according to the Committee for Economic Development, "Fully two-thirds of the public think that their own representative in Congress would listen to the views of outsiders who made large political contributions before a constituent's views."[9]

For their part, lobbyists, CEOs, and wealthy individuals alike all have candidly admitted donating substantial sums of soft money to national committees not on ideological grounds, but for the purpose of securing influence over federal officials.[10] One lobbyist who had testified said, "Ordinarily, people feel inclined to reciprocate favors. Do a bigger favor for someone— that is, write a larger check—and they feel even more compelled to reciprocate."[11]

Although the U.S. Supreme Court initially upheld the ban on soft-money contributions in 2003,[12] it is not clear whether the ban will continue to withstand legal challenges. Individuals and groups who oppose the ban have continued to challenge it, and an ideologically divided U.S. Supreme Court appears willing to revisit its election law decisions. The Court, in fact, overturned its own 1990 decision to strike down an unrelated provision of BCRA in 2010.[13]

Unlimited individual campaign contributions defeat the principle of "one person, one vote."

Campaign finance reformers are not only concerned with corporate soft-money donations but also with the effect of individual contributions by wealthy donors. Part of the compromise that led to passage of BCRA was an increase in the limit that an individual can contribute to a candidate in a federal election, from $1,000 to $2,000, but at the same time, such restrictions were extended to individual contributions to political parties. Opponents of campaign finance restrictions, however, ask whether any limits should be placed on the amount of money a person can give to a candidate (or a political party). There have been a number of court challenges to the individual donation limits for federal elections, and many have challenged state contribution limits, both in court and in the state legislatures.

Like corporate soft money, individual contributions to political parties received a great deal of negative attention during the 1996 elections. President Bill Clinton's opponents charged him with selling access to the White House in exchange for contributions to the Democratic Party. People who attended White House coffees had frequently contributed tens of thousands of dollars. But scandal really broke out when the media revealed that several people, each of whom had contributed hundreds of thousands of dollars to the Democratic National Committee, were invited to sleep in the historic Lincoln Bedroom at the White House.

Although critics charged that Clinton was abusing both his elected office and the sanctity of the White House, the Clinton administration denied that it was running a hotel service for wealthy contributors and maintained that no laws were broken. The scandal was repeated in 2000, when Clinton, already on his way out of the White House, opened the Lincoln Bedroom to people who had donated money to Democratic causes while his wife, Hillary, was running for a Senate seat in New York.

Scandals such as this helped to gain support for BCRA's limits on individual donations to political parties.

Another controversial issue is regulating who could donate money to candidates and who could not. During early deliberations about BCRA, some suggested restricting the amount of money that a candidate for the Senate or House of Representatives could raise from out of state. While only residents of Georgia, for example, may vote for that state's senators and representatives, federal law does not prohibit residents of other states from contributing money to candidates in Georgia's congressional elections.

Events during the 2002 congressional elections demonstrated that out-of-state money plays a large role in determining the outcome of elections. During primary elections in Alabama and Georgia, incumbent representatives Earl Hilliard and Cynthia McKinney lost the Democratic Party's nominations (and therefore their seats) to challengers who benefited greatly from out-of-state money. In both cases, the incumbent and the victor were each African American; in both cases, a majority of the voters in the district were African American. Both campaigns, however, attracted significant donations from people who were neither African American nor residents of these states. According to the *Montgomery Advertiser*, Hilliard's challenger, Artur Davis, raised just over $306,000 in individual contributions, and nearly $189,000 of these contributions came from New York. McKinney's challenger, Denise Majette, also raised a significant amount of out-of-state money.[14]

The reason the races attracted so much money from out of state was that Hilliard and McKinney had both taken anti-Israel positions, angering many Jewish people across the nation. Journalist Jonathan Rosenblum extolled, "Jewish political activists scored impressive victories in two recent congressional primaries," noting that a majority of the funding for Hilliard's and McKinney's challengers had come from "out-of-state Jewish contributors."[15] Many applauded the defeats, pleased that an organized effort had removed two anti-Israel votes from the House of Representatives.

Not everyone agreed that this was a case of democracy working properly. Many people were concerned that the outcome of races between two black candidates in African-American districts were so heavily influenced by non-African-American contributors, according to the leader of the Congressional Black Caucus, Representative Eddie Bernice Johnson, a Texas Democrat. She expressed concern that many black citizens feel as though "Jewish people are attempting to pick our leaders."[16]

A broader concern is that interest groups can selectively "buy" seats in Congress by targeting elections in which the candidates would otherwise not be able to raise significant campaign funds—for example in less affluent or less populous districts or states. This raises the question of whether an official so elected would represent his or her constituents or the people who paid for his or her campaign. Would Davis and Majette be willing to take a position that is popular with African-American voters in the South but unpopular with potential Jewish contributors in New York?

Campaign contributions are not "free speech" deserving of full First Amendment protection.

Opponents of campaign finance reform have attacked the Supreme Court's ruling in *Buckley v. Valeo* that political contributions receive a lesser level of protection under the First Amendment than either political speech or expenditures on advertising about political issues. Reformers support the holding in *Buckley*, however, maintaining that an important distinction exists between political speech and the infusion of money into politics.

In support of the BCRA's provisions limiting soft-money contributions, a coalition of former leaders of the American Civil Liberties Union (ACLU) argued:

The First Amendment is designed to promote a functioning and fair democracy. The current system of campaign financing makes a mockery of that ideal by enabling wealthy and powerful interests effectively

FROM THE BENCH

Buckley v. Valeo, 424 U.S. 1 (1976)

[A] limitation upon the amount that any one person or group may contribute to a candidate or political committee entails only a marginal restriction upon the contributor's ability to engage in free communication. A contribution serves as a general expression of support for the candidate and his views, but does not communicate the underlying basis for the support. The quantity of communication by the contributor does not increase perceptibly with the size of his contribution, since the expression rests solely on the undifferentiated, symbolic act of contributing. At most, the size of the contribution provides a very rough index of the intensity of the contributor's support for the candidate. A limitation on the amount of money a person may give to a candidate or campaign organization thus involves little direct restraint on his political communication, for it permits the symbolic expression of support evidenced by a contribution but does not in any way infringe the contributor's freedom to discuss candidates and issues. While contributions may result in political expression if spent by a candidate or an association to present views to the voters, the transformation of contributions into political debate involves speech by someone other than the contributor.

Given the important role of contributions in financing political campaigns, contribution restrictions could have a severe impact on political dialogue if the limitations prevented candidates and political committees from amassing the resources necessary for effective advocacy. There is no indication, however, that the contribution limitations imposed by the Act would have any dramatic adverse effect on the funding of campaigns and political associations. The overall effect of the Act's contribution ceilings is merely to require candidates and political committees to raise funds from a greater number of persons and to compel people who would otherwise contribute amounts greater than the statutory limits to expend such funds on direct political expression, rather than to reduce the total amount of money potentially available to promote political expression.

to set the national agenda.... [W]hen the government intervenes to restore the integrity of the democratic process, it enhances, rather than retards, First
Amendment interests.[17]

Although the ACLU itself opposed BCRA, the fact that
former leaders of the organization took a position arguing for
a narrow interpretation of the First Amendment is particularly
remarkable: Throughout the years, the ACLU has argued that
the First Amendment's protections are almost boundless and
that pornography, flag burning, and Ku Klux Klan marches
are—despite their repugnancy to much of the population—all
protected forms of expression.

It appears that the U.S. Supreme Court continues to give
diminished First Amendment protection, but those protections
might be expanding. In the 2006 *Randall v. Sorrell*[18] decision, the
Court struck down a Vermont law limiting both total spending
by the candidates and individual and political party contributions to a candidate in a state election. An individual could not
contribute more than $400 to a candidate for governor or other
statewide office, more than $300 for a candidate for state sena-
tor, or $200 for state representative. Political parties were subject
to the same limit, so that, altogether, local, state, and national
branches of the Democratic Party could contribute no more
than $400 to a Democratic candidate for governor. Although the
Supreme Court had upheld contribution limits in the past, these
were too restrictive, the Court held.

In a dissent, Justice David Souter argued that, although
the contribution limits seemed small, they were justified by the
findings of the Vermont legislature on how to keep money from
corrupting state politics:

To place Vermont's contribution limits beyond the constitutional pale, therefore, is to forget . . . our self-admonition
against second-guessing legislative judgments about the

risk of corruption to which contribution limits have to be fitted. . . . Vermont's legislators themselves testified at length about the money that gets their special attention . . . (some candidates and elected officials, particularly when time is limited, respond and give access to contributors who make large contributions in preference to those who make small or no contributions); (testimony of Elizabeth Ready: "If I have only got an hour at night when I get home to return calls, I am much more likely to return [a donor's] call than I would [a non-donor's]. . . . [W]hen you only have a few minutes to talk, there are certain people that get access."). . . . The limits set by the legislature . . . accurately reflect the level of contribution considered suspiciously large by the Vermont public.[19]

Justice Souter also quoted the lower court's findings that money was not necessary for campaigning, suggesting that contributions only served to obligate the candidate to the donor:

In the context of Vermont politics, $200, $300, and $400 donations are clearly large, as the legislature determined. Small donations are considered to be strong acts of political support in this state. William Meub testified that a contribution of $1 is meaningful because it represents a commitment by the contributor that is likely to become a vote for the candidate. Gubernatorial candidate Ruth Dwyer values the small contributions of $5 so much that she personally sends thank you notes to those donors. . . . In Vermont, many politicians have run effective and winning campaigns with very little money, and some with no money at all. . . . In Vermont legislative races, low-cost methods such as door-to-door campaigning are standard and even expected by the voters.[20]

Summary

The Bipartisan Campaign Reform Act of 2002 was a response to widespread concerns that money is corrupting American democracy. Corporations, unions, special interest groups, and wealthy individuals have pumped millions of dollars into election campaigns, causing many to wonder whether politicians represent the interest of the voters or the big-time contributors. With numerous court challenges to BCRA and debates continuing at the state level, the dispute over campaign finance reform will continue for years to come.

Campaign Contributions Are Political Speech

Although many recent polls indicate that Americans have lost faith in their elected officials, and although the Bipartisan Campaign Reform Act (BCRA) passed in 2002 with the support of both major parties, not everyone supports campaign finance "reform." In fact, many people believe that campaign finance restrictions actually harm the democratic process.

Many politicians and members of the media act as though it is a foregone conclusion that there is too much money in politics: Recall the article comparing the cost of the New York governor's race to burgers and fries. Others, however, use the same analogy to claim that not enough money is spent on campaigning. In 2000, journalist Tom Bethell wrote: "In the latest election cycle, $675 million was spent contesting House and Senate seats. With 196 million eligible votes, this is less than $4 a head, or, as Sen. [Mitch] McConnell [R.-Ky.] likes to say, less than the price of a

McDonald's extra value meal."[1] In the senator's opinion, the cost of a fast-food meal is evidently a reasonable price for educating voters about campaign issues.

When compared to the overall amount of money that Congress spends each year, the amount of money spent on political campaigns seems even less significant. As Bethell points out, in 1998 Senate races, winning candidates spent an average of just under $5 million each. To Bethell, this seems like a wise investment: "Congress spends about $1.7 trillion a year, and each senator will be in office for six years. Thus $5 million 'buys' a one-hundredth share of control over the disposition of about $10 trillion."[2]

People like Bethell are not seriously suggesting that a political campaign is a financial investment like purchasing stocks and bonds. Many supporters of soft money feel that banning it ignores the real problem of American politics—that the federal government spends far too much money and regulates businesses too strictly. In the words of the Cato Institute's Doug Bandow: "As long as Uncle Sam hands out nearly $2 trillion in loot every year and uses its rule-making power to enrich or impoverish entire industries, individuals and companies will spend millions to influence the process."[3]

Opponents of campaign finance restrictions opposed BCRA in Congress and continue to challenge the law in the courts. They believe that the system of soft money actually aids democracy by helping to maintain political parties, that individual contributions allow people to participate fully in government, and that limits on campaign contributions violate the First Amendment by restricting freedom of speech.

Contributions to political parties are an essential part of the political process.

Opponents of campaign finance restrictions believe that soft-money contributions are an important part of the political process, chiefly because they benefit the American political party system. For the past two centuries, each president of the United States has been elected with the backing of a major political party. Since the Civil War, the Democratic and Republican parties have dominated national politics.

Many people believe that voter apathy and declining confidence in the political system can be traced to a decline in support for the major parties—a decline that will become worse if the ban on soft-money contributions to political parties continues to be enforced. Political science professor Steven E. Schier believes that experience in the United States and elsewhere demonstrates that political parties are necessary for democracy to thrive. He writes: "Throughout American history, political parties have performed vital services for our democracy. . . . Most of the world's democracies that have survived for 25 years or more have had stable party systems with a low number of parties."[4] Proponents of the party system have developed a number of theories as to how the party system supports democracy.

One way is that political parties unite members of society behind political issues. A citizen who supports and trusts a particular political party does not have to study complicated issues such as environmental regulations and health-care programs—not to mention election law—or carefully analyze each candidate's position on every issue. Political parties make voting much simpler, Schier writes, "encouraging those with less education and less income to vote. . . . Choosing between two teams rather than among a plethora of individual candidates makes it easier for more citizens to cast an informed vote."[5]

Political parties have played a major role in registering voters and getting them to the polls. In fact, the soft-money system originally developed as a way for interest groups, corporations, and unions to financially support what Senator Russ Feingold has called "party-building activities such as get-out-the-vote campaigns and voter-registration drives."[6] Many people agree that such efforts are necessary to encourage more people to vote; however, it will be more difficult for parties to conduct these activities if the soft-money ban is enforced. Attorney Allison R. Hayward writes, "[S]pecial-interest groups, corporations, and unions . . . could also engage in voter-registration activities once pursued by parties, but one should doubt that interest groups would pursue these activities on the same scale as parties."[7] Sponsoring these activities individually would not be as efficient as allowing these organizations to contribute soft money to the parties to do them.

Another beneficial aspect of the party system that is hampered by the soft-money ban is the major role that political parties play in helping new candidates challenge incumbents. In many states, a single party dominates politics, which makes fundraising for opposing parties difficult because people do not want to contribute to what they see as a losing cause. In other states, politicians have represented their constituencies for decades, and challengers have difficulties overcoming the incumbent's name recognition. In such states, voters often feel as though they have no choice in selecting their government officials. In South Carolina, for example, Strom Thurmond held on to his Senate seat for more than 45 years until retiring in January 2003 at age 100. Although many people opposed Thurmond, who had run for president in 1948 under the slogan "Segregation Forever," the opposition was never strong enough to unseat him.

With access to soft money, national political parties were able to help their candidates campaign, even if there was strong local opposition. John Samples of the Cato Institute writes, "America needs more competition: About 98 percent of congressional incumbents get reelected. Soft money can help challengers compete with incumbents. Parties make sure soft money ends up where it's needed most."[8]

Although the soft-money ban was promoted as an anticorruption measure, some people believe that the soft-money system actually *decreases* the possibility of corruption by isolating elected officials from political contributors. Many people believe that, regardless of campaign finance legislation, politicians will

In 1948, Governor Strom Thurmond of South Carolina *(at podium)* ran for president on a racial segregation platform. Despite his controversial views, Thurmond later became a U.S. senator and served in that office for nearly a half century, demonstrating how difficult it can be to unseat an incumbent politician.

continue to find new ways of financing their campaigns. If these methods were to rely exclusively on direct contributions to candidates, politicians would more likely feel obligated to these contributors. On the other hand, under the soft-money system, when contributions come to a national political party, which can use the funds for any of hundreds of candidates, the chance that any one candidate will feel obligated to the contributor is reduced. Calling soft-money contributions "a buffer against corruption," Samples writes, "The winners are beholden to their party and not to individual donors. Soft money is actually less of a danger than money given directly to a candidate's campaign."[9]

Additionally, while banning soft money might limit the influence of corporations and wealthy individuals, the ban will allow others even greater influence in the political process. For example, even though the soft-money ban covers labor unions, the Cato Institute's Bandow believes that the ban actually gives unions an unfair advantage over other interest groups, such as corporations, because unions "often deploy legions of volunteers" for campaign and election activities.[10]

Similarly, it is undisputed that the news media, especially television and newspapers, have an enormous influence over the outcome of elections. The media can have a huge impact on voters' choices by endorsing particular candidates or by running coverage favorable or unfavorable to particular candidates—such as reporting just before the 2000 election that George W. Bush had been arrested many years earlier for drunken driving. By limiting the financial resources of political parties to run advertisements, Bethell writes, enforcement of a soft-money ban "would increase the media's power by restricting alternative sources of information."[11]

Contributions by individuals are an essential part of the political process.

Opponents of campaign finance restrictions believe placing constraints on the amount of money that an individual can contribute to candidates limits that person's participation in the democratic process. For example, while a person might not have time to go door-to-door canvassing on behalf of a political candidate, the person might have enough money to donate to the campaign to help the candidate hire canvassers. By limiting the ability of individual citizens to make campaign contributions, state and federal election laws limit their citizens' voice in politics.

In a 2006 case, Supreme Court Justice Antonin Scalia argued that speech and money are inseparable in modern society:

> In any economy operated on even the most rudimentary principles of division of labor, effective public communication requires the speaker to make use of the services of others. An author may write a novel, but he will seldom publish and distribute it himself. A freelance reporter may write a story, but he will rarely edit, print, and deliver it to subscribers.[12]

While many criticized the role of out-of-state Jewish contributors in helping to defeat Earl Hilliard and Cynthia McKinney, two Southern African-American politicians, others thought that their defeat was a lesson in democracy. Michael Barone writes that the reason Hilliard and McKinney lost was not simply because out-of-state contributors had supported their challengers, Artur Davis and Denise Majette; rather: "Majette and Davis couldn't win unless their issue stands were acceptable to most primary voters. You can spend a lot of money and still lose if the product you're selling isn't acceptable."[13] In Barone's opinion, Hilliard and McKinney lost because they took extreme positions on Israel, terrorism, and other issues; out-of-state contributions merely helped the challengers publicize these positions.

Restrictions on political contributions violate the First Amendment.

Some people have taken the passage of BCRA as a means of challenging one of the central holdings of *Buckley v. Valeo*—that the federal government, acting consistently with the First Amendment, may limit campaign contributions more closely than it may regulate expenditures on political speech.

While the Court upheld individual campaign contribution limits in *McConnell v. FEC*, it did signal some hesitation about restrictions in free speech in a later case. In *Randall v. Sorrell*, the case in which the Court invalidated Vermont's $200 to $400 contribution limits, the justices could not agree on their rationale for striking down the law. Several justices, including Stephen Breyer, Samuel Alito, and Chief Justice Roberts, found that the limits were too low and therefore placed too great a burden on free speech. Justice Clarence Thomas, however, did not think the Court went far enough. In an opinion joined by Justice Scalia, he wrote that any limits on political contributions were an improper restriction of free speech:

> An individual's First Amendment right is infringed whether his speech is decreased by 5% or 95%, and whether he suffers alone or shares his violation with his fellow citizens. Certainly, the First Amendment does not authorize us to judge whether a restriction of political speech imposes a sufficiently severe disadvantage on challengers that a candidate should be able to complain.[14]

In a separate opinion, Justice Scalia argued that restrictions on campaign contributions allow the government to silence opposition candidates, whom fewer people support:

> To a government bent on suppressing speech, this mode of organization presents opportunities: Control any cog in the machine, and you can halt the whole apparatus. License printers, and it matters little whether authors are still free to write. Restrict the sale of books, and it matters little who prints them. Predictably, repressive regimes have exploited these principles by attacking all levels of the production and dissemination of ideas.[15]

Many others have challenged the Court's distinction between political speech and political spending, because it is clear that political speech costs money. Attorney Erik S. Jaffe and the Cato

Institute's Robert A. Levy believe that it is inconsistent to think that the Constitution protects the exercise of a particular right, but not paying money for the exercise of that right. They write: "The right to speak . . . encompasses the right to pay for speech . . . just as the right to legal counsel encompasses the right to hire a lawyer, and the right to free exercise of religion includes the right to contribute to the church of one's choice."[16]

Many opponents of campaign finance restrictions also believe that the soft-money ban is too broad because it places too many restrictions on the speech of political parties. The purported rationale behind the soft-money ban is to limit election communications—something the Court held was constitutional in *Buckley*. The soft-money ban, however, goes much further than that. The ban makes it much more difficult for political parties to engage in legitimate party activities, such as voter-registration drives.

Opponents of the soft-money ban believe that the underlying motivation of "reformers"—elimination of corruption—is suspect. They feel that there is no real proof that soft money has led to any specific improper acts and that the "perception" of corruption is not a valid enough reason to limit contributions to parties. In the *McConnell* lawsuit challenging the constitutionality of BCRA, the Cato Institute and the Institute for Justice argued that, while fighting "actual corruption" is an important goal, the federal government should not suppress any kind of political expression—such as soft-money contributions—that has not been proven to lead to actual corruption. In an amicus (friend-of-the-court) brief, the groups argued: "[T]he proper answer to such misperception is either more speech, the election of candidates voluntarily practicing the public's notion of virtue, or, ultimately, a constitutional amendment if the existing system cannot hold the public's confidence."[17] In other words, if the public thinks that politicians are corrupt, then the answer is for the public to vote the politicians out of office; the answer is not for the government to suppress political debate.

QUOTABLE

Justice Clarence Thomas

In a dissenting opinion, Justice Thomas declared that campaign finance reform violates the First Amendment:

Political speech is the primary object of First Amendment protection. . . . The Founders sought to protect the rights of individuals to engage in political speech because a self-governing people depends upon the free exchange of political information. And that free exchange should receive the most protection when it matters the most—during campaigns for elective office. . . .

For nearly half a century, this Court has extended First Amendment protection to a multitude of forms of "speech," such as making false defamatory statements, filing lawsuits, dancing nude, exhibiting drive-in movies with nudity, burning flags, and wearing military uniforms. Not surprisingly, the Courts of Appeals have followed our lead and concluded that the First Amendment protects, for example, begging, shouting obscenities, erecting tables on a sidewalk, and refusing to wear a necktie. . . . Whatever the proper status of such activities under the First Amendment, I am confident that they are less integral to the functioning of our Republic than campaign contributions. . . .

The decision of individuals to speak through contributions . . . is entirely reasonable. . . . Campaign organizations offer a ready-built, convenient means of communicating for donors wishing to support and amplify political messages. Furthermore, the leader of the organization—the candidate—has a strong self-interest in efficiently expending funds in a manner that maximizes the power of the messages the contributor seeks to disseminate. Individual citizens understandably realize that they "may add more to political discourse by giving rather than spending, if the donee is able to put the funds to more productive use than can the individual." . . .

Even for the affluent, the added costs in money or time of taking out a newspaper advertisement, handing out leaflets on the street, or standing in front of one's house with a handheld sign may make the difference between participating and not participating in some public debate. . . .

Source: *Nixon v. Shrink Missouri Government PAC*, No. 98-963 (January 24, 2000) (Thomas, J., dissenting).

Summary

Though Congress passed the Bipartisan Campaign Reform Act of 2002 with widespread support, opponents have challenged the law as unconstitutional. Not everyone agrees that there is too much money in politics; many believe that the party system is essential to democracy and that parties need money to survive. Similarly, campaign contributions allow people to express their political views.

Regulating Television Promotes Fair Campaigns

In the months leading up to the 1988 presidential election, Governor Michael Dukakis of Massachusetts, the Democratic candidate, was vigorously competing with Vice President George H.W. Bush, the Republican candidate. The Dukakis campaign fell apart, however, after a series of television commercials attacked his record as governor. The first advertisement, sponsored by an independent political action committee—not the Bush campaign—introduced Americans to a person who would become permanently linked with Dukakis: Willie Horton.

Portraying Dukakis as "soft on crime," the advertisements showed the mug shot of Horton, a convicted murderer who had received numerous short "furloughs" from prison under a program that Dukakis strongly supported. During one furlough, Horton kidnapped and assaulted a young couple, raping the woman. The ads generated a great deal of media coverage, with

Horton's victims appearing on a number of high-profile television programs. Soon after, Bush's campaign launched its own set of advertisements, attacking Dukakis's record on crime, but without mentioning Horton specifically.

In *Checkbook Democracy*, political science professor Darrell M. West writes that the two-pronged attack—with an independent group running ads linking Dukakis to Horton and the Bush campaign running ads with general criticism of Dukakis's policy—worked extremely well for Bush. He was able to paint a very negative picture of Dukakis without being criticized for running a negative campaign. More significantly, West writes that the ads benefited Bush by "arous[ing] racial fears" among Americans: "Republicans had picked the perfect racial offense, that of a black felon raping a white woman."[1]

Bush won the election by a comfortable margin, but many, recalling the Horton ad, questioned whether his tactics were fair. Certainly, it was a legitimate concern that the furlough program Dukakis supported had allowed a convicted murderer sentenced to life to leave prison and commit other crimes. Many, however, felt that the proper way for Bush to inform voters of this concern would have been to take up the issue in a debate or at least to deliver the criticisms in his own voice without hiding behind an anonymous attack ad.

Attack ads harm democracy by distorting the real issues.

While the "Willie Horton" advertising campaign was not the first occurrence of negative campaigning in American politics, some people think that the advertisements opened the door for a new style of campaigning, in which politicians ignored the real issues and instead attacked the other candidate's personal character or distorted the other candidate's positions.

In Montana's senatorial race in 2002, Republican challenger Mike Taylor pulled out of the race after the Democratic incumbent candidate, Senator Max Baucus, ran a controversial television ad. The advertisement accused Taylor of running a "student loan scam" during the 1980s. Taylor admitted that his hairstyling schools had made some bookkeeping errors and had repaid the federal government $27,000, but he said that he had admitted his errors and made good on the discrepancy and that the settlement agreement did not include any admission of wrongdoing. Therefore, Taylor said, the accusation of his running a "student loan scam" was very misleading.

Even more misleading, Taylor's campaign manager told the *Great Falls Tribune*, was that the ad "insinuates that Mike Taylor is a gay hairdresser." As described by the article, the ad showed actual video footage, from a television program on which Taylor appeared, "of a bearded Taylor from nearly 20 years ago, dressed in flamboyant 1970s-era clothing and applying face cream to a male model."[2] Although the ad showed actual footage of Taylor's television show, many attacked the Democratic campaign for appealing to antigay prejudices, much as the Willie Horton ads had appealed to racial prejudices in 1988. With commercials such as these, the damage is difficult to control once the cat is out of the bag. After withdrawing from the race, Taylor said that he would have had to "blanket the airwaves with slime" to counteract Baucus's accusations of fraud and insinuations of homosexuality.[3]

Another criticism that many people have is that attack ads are often designed as an anonymous attack on a person's character. One of the biggest criticisms of the Willie Horton advertising campaign was that the ads attacked Dukakis by appealing to racial prejudice; had Bush attempted such tactics, the public might have branded him a racist, but because the ads were relatively anonymous, Bush benefited from them without being linked with the message.

In the view of many people, the First Amendment was designed to protect public debate, not anonymous attacks on a person's character. For years, Congress has carefully regulated campaign advertisements, requiring that the advertisements disclose the source of their funding. (In the 1976 *Buckley v. Valeo* decision, the Supreme Court ruled that the federal government could regulate any advertisement that "expressly advocates the election or defeat of a clearly identified candidate."[4]) In the years leading up to the passage of the Bipartisan Campaign Reform Act (BCRA), however, many groups skirted this requirement by running advertisements attacking the candidate without explicitly advising people to vote against the candidate: Such ads escaped federal regulation of campaign advertising, and therefore the sponsors of the ads were not identified.

Although the sponsors of such advertisements have claimed that they are "issue ads," they are often campaign advertisements that have little to do with issues. Arguing in support of BCRA's ban on "sham issue advertisements," a coalition of former ACLU leaders gave an example of an anonymous "issue" ad that was clearly a campaign advertisement—it began to run two weeks before a congressional election:

> Who is Bill Yellowtail? He preaches family values but took a swing at his wife. . . . He talks law and order . . . but is himself a convicted felon. And though he talks about protecting children, Yellowtail failed to make his own child support payments—then voted against child support enforcement. Call Bill Yellowtail. Tell him to support family values.[5]

Despite their obvious attempt to influence an election, the sponsors of this advertisement claimed that it was not a campaign ad subject to federal regulation. The former ACLU leaders argued:

> The increased use of such advertisements has undermined the [law] . . . and allowed other individuals and entities to fund . . . advertisements without disclosing their identities or providing the electorate with crucial

information regarding funding sources to enable the electorate to make informed federal election choices.[6]

Without such a ban, racist groups like the Ku Klux Klan, for example, could advertise in favor of a certain candidate, and the public would never know.

BCRA included measures limiting attack ads, extending the definition of "electioneering communications" subject to federal regulations to include any advertisement referring to a "clearly identified candidate for Federal office" within 30 days of a primary election or 60 days of a general election.[7] Supporters of the legislation had hoped that the provision would close the loophole in federal election law that allowed anonymous advertisers to attack candidates for office using "sham issue ads." While the Supreme Court initially upheld these restrictions on issue ads in the 2003 case *McConnell v. FEC*, it backtracked on its ruling a few years later in *FEC v. Wisconsin Right to Life*.

In that case, a split majority of justices upheld the right of an anti-abortion group to run advertisements urging Wisconsin residents to call their senators and tell them to speed up the consideration of judicial nominees, many of whom were anti-abortion:

> A group of senators is using the filibuster delay tactic to block federal judicial nominees from a simple "yes" or "no" vote. So qualified candidates don't get a chance to serve.
>
> It's politics at work, causing gridlock and backing up some of our courts to a state of emergency.
>
> Contact Senators Feingold and Kohl and tell them to oppose the filibuster.[8]

Because the ad did not mention that Senator Feingold was up for reelection and did not explicitly state that he was one of the senators responsible for the delay tactic, the Court ruled that the ads could not be regulated as election ads. In his dissent, Justice David Souter, however, argued that the ruling would undermine the ban on corporate campaign contributions because it essentially allows corporations to spend money on candidates' behalf:

> After today, the ban on [direct] contributions [to campaigns] by corporations and unions and the limitation on their corrosive spending when they enter the political arena are open to easy circumvention, and the possibilities for regulating corporate and union campaign money are unclear. The ban on [direct] contributions will mean nothing much, now that companies and unions can save candidates the expense of advertising directly, simply by running "issue ads" without express advocacy, or by funneling the money through an independent corporation like WRTL.[9]

It became even easier for corporations to run attack ads in 2010, when the U.S. Supreme Court ruled in *Citizens United v. FEC*[10] that provisions of BCRA banning corporate expenditures on campaign advertising were unconstitutional. Thus, a corporation can now run campaign ads directly—as long as the corporation discloses its identity—rather than through independent organizations or political action committees.

The proliferation of television advertisements interferes with meaningful election coverage.

To many campaign reformers, the problem of television advertising is not limited to attack ads that distort the issues. There is also the problem of lucrative ad sales that encourage stations to provide even less coverage of campaign issues. Rather than having local news programs explore political issues in greater detail or setting aside time for debates, television stations simply sell more advertising time to politicians. Senator Russ Feingold commented:

Although broadcast advertising is one of the most effective forms of communication in our democracy, it also diminishes the quality of our electoral process in two ways. First, broadcasters often fail to provide adequate coverage to the issues in elections, focusing instead on the horse race, if they cover elections at all. Second, the extraordinarily high cost of advertising time fuels the insatiable need for candidates to spend more and more time fund-raising instead of talking with voters. These two problems interact to undermine the great promise that television has for promoting democratic discourse in our country.[11]

THE LETTER OF THE LAW

Bipartisan Campaign Reform Act (2002)

The following is an excerpt of the law's definition of campaign advertisements. While such ads are no longer prohibited, the sponsors of the ads are required to identify themselves:

(3) ELECTIONEERING COMMUNICATION.—For purposes of this subsection—

    (A) IN GENERAL.—

(i) The term "electioneering communication" means any broadcast, cable, or satellite communication which—

    (I) refers to a clearly identified candidate for Federal office;

    (II) is made within—

        (aa) 60 days before a general, special, or run-off election for the office sought by the candidate; or

        (bb) 30 days before a primary or preference election, or a convention or caucus of a political party that has authority to nominate a candidate, for the office sought by the candidate; and

(III) in the case of a communication which refers to a candidate for an office other than President or Vice President, is targeted to the relevant electorate.

Many people believe that it might be possible for candidates to make some valid points on certain issues during a 30-second television advertisement—for example, Candidate A might run an ad criticizing Candidate B for her past votes to raise taxes. People who see the ad would not know the whole story, however: Perhaps Candidate B voted to raise taxes to rescue failing public schools or for some other reason that voters might support. Most political issues are extremely complicated and cannot be discussed in a 30-second commercial.

Journalist Jeffrey H. Birnbaum believes that voters would learn much more and be able to make informed decisions if they watched programming in which candidates discussed the issues in more depth—such as "minidebates, interviews, or even straightforward statements read on the air by the candidates themselves ... programming that would inform voters about the upcoming election by using the candidates themselves."[12] As a successful example of such a strategy, Birnbaum cites the surprise election of former professional wrestler Jesse "The Body" Ventura as Minnesota's governor in 1998. After television stations in Minnesota's largest cities aired two-minute messages by the candidates and the League of Women Voters arranged a debate that was carried statewide, Ventura beat both the Democratic and Republican candidates in an election that attracted many new voters. Birnbaum called what happened in Minnesota a "model of how to avoid superficial TV coverage of a campaign."[13]

Unfortunately, reformers say, in most of the rest of the country, broadcasters are not so willing to carry debates and other programs examining issues in depth. Senator Feingold lamented:

> [O]nly 18 percent of gubernatorial, senatorial, and congressional debates held in 2000 were televised by network TV, and an additional 18 percent were covered by PBS or small independent stations. More than 63 percent were

not televised at all. This is shocking in a democracy that depends on information and open debate.[14]

Free airtime and televised debates for candidates would benefit voters.

The answer to the lack of meaningful candidate programming, campaign reformers say, is to require broadcasters to carry the type of programming that the Minnesota stations carried when Ventura was running for office. To that end, Senator John McCain and Senator Feingold, following up on BCRA, proposed requiring television stations to carry two hours of political programming per week in the weeks leading up to a federal election. Without such a requirement, they argued, most stations would continue to shun meaningful election coverage. In economic terms, it makes sense for profit-seeking television stations to sell advertising time to candidates: the less "free" coverage the stations provide, the more advertising spots they can sell.

To campaign reformers, however, the issue is not so simple. Citing the principle that the airwaves are a public trust, they argue that the stations have a duty to provide programming in the public interest. In 2002, Senator McCain argued: "[There is a] long history of requiring broadcasters to serve the public interest in exchange for the privilege of obtaining an exclusive license to use a scarce public resource: the electromagnetic spectrum."[15] Each television set sold has a limited number of channels that can pick up television broadcasts through the airwaves—as opposed to through cable or satellite television. Television channels correspond to different "wavelengths" of electromagnetic radiation—the same type of invisible radiation that carries radio stations and cell phone and cordless phone conversations. Television stations do not "use up" a particular wavelength: In theory, one town could have 10 stations, all broadcasting on Channel Five. The obvious problem is that—if 10 stations were on the same channel—nobody could watch any of them because they would all interfere with each other.

Therefore, the federal government grants each television station an exclusive license to use a particular channel in a particular area. In the words of Senator Feingold, "The public owns the airwaves and licenses them to broadcasters. Broadcasters pay nothing for their use of this scarce and very valuable public resource. Their only 'payment' is a promise to meet public interest standards, a promise that often goes unfulfilled."[16] Throughout the history of television, the government has used the public interest rationale to require that television stations air "public service announcements," such as reminders from the fire department to check smoke detector batteries. The same rationale explains why broadcast television stations have agreed not to use explicit language or graphic sex and violence.

Supporters of free airtime proposals believe that the public interest rationale strongly favors free airtime for political candidates. They note that the imposition on broadcasters—two hours per week for six weeks—is very reasonable compared to the immense value of a broadcast license. Senator McCain said, "The burden imposed on broadcasters pales in comparison to the enormous value of the spectrum, which recent estimates suggest is worth as much as $367 billion."[17]

Supporters note that free airtime has been successful in places in which it has been tried. Ric Bainter and Paul Lhevine have praised Seattle's efforts to persuade television stations to air the "Video Voter Guide," in which each candidate has three minutes to address the public. They write, "Seattle continues to lead the way in campaign finance work and sets a clear example for others to follow."[18]

Still, despite such promise, Congress has taken no action on a free airtime bill since Senators McCain and Feingold first proposed one almost a decade ago. Broadcasters and opponents of campaign reform have criticized laws restricting attack ads and proposals to give candidates free airtime on First Amendment grounds. Although the First Amendment prohibits Congress from passing any laws "abridging the freedom of speech,"

FROM THE BENCH

Red Lion Broadcasting Co. v. FCC, 395 U.S. 367 (1969)

In this case, the U.S. Supreme Court ruled that the scarcity of the broadcast spectrum allows for government regulation of radio and television:

> Although broadcasting is clearly a medium affected by a First Amendment interest ... differences in the characteristics of new media justify differences in the First Amendment standards applied to them. ...
>
> [B]ecause the frequencies reserved for public broadcasting were limited in number, it was essential for the Government to tell some applicants that they could not broadcast at all because there was room for only a few.
>
> Where there are substantially more individuals who want to broadcast than there are frequencies to allocate, it is idle to posit an unabridgeable First Amendment right to broadcast comparable to the right of every individual to speak, write, or publish. If 100 persons want broadcast licenses but there are only 10 frequencies to allocate, all of them may have the same "right" to a license; but if there is to be any effective communication by radio, only a few can be licensed and the rest must be barred from the airwaves. ...
>
> [As] far as the First Amendment is concerned, those who are licensed stand no better than those to whom licenses are refused. A license permits broadcasting, but the licensee has no constitutional right to be the one who holds the license or to monopolize a radio frequency to the exclusion of his fellow citizens. There is nothing in the First Amendment which prevents the Government from requiring a licensee to share his frequency with others and to conduct himself as a proxy or fiduciary with obligations to present those views and voices which are representative of his community and which would otherwise, by necessity, be barred from the airwaves. ...
>
> [The] people as a whole retain their interest in free speech by radio and their collective right to have the medium function consistently with the ends and purposes of the First Amendment. It is the right of the viewers and listeners, not the right of the broadcasters, which is paramount. ... It is the purpose of the First Amendment to preserve an uninhibited marketplace of ideas in which truth will ultimately prevail, rather than to countenance monopolization of that market, whether it be by the Government itself or a private licensee.

campaign reformers have maintained that regulating the use of a public resource as valuable as the airwaves does not impinge upon free speech. Rather, it is similar to requiring people to obtain a permit to hold an event in a public place—something that the Supreme Court has said is not a violation of First Amendment rights.

Summary

Many attribute low voter turnout to the way campaigns are typically conducted: 30-second ads attacking one of the candidates, with most voters learning very little about the real issues. A 2010 U.S. Supreme Court decision made it even easier for corporations to sponsor attack ads, leaving campaign reformers searching for new ways to make elections fairer. They would like to see more in-depth campaign coverage on television and have even suggested requiring television stations to provide candidates with free airtime.

Regulating Television Is Unconstitutional and Undemocratic

So-called attack ads might not be friendly, but they are certainly nothing new. Florida's senatorial election of 1950 provides perhaps the most humorous example of dirty campaigning. Reportedly, challenger George Smathers called incumbent Claude Pepper a "shameless extrovert" who "matriculated" while he was in college and practiced "celibacy" before marriage. These claims were absolutely true and absolutely innocuous—but sounded dirty to people who were unfamiliar with the terms. (An extrovert is a person with an outgoing personality; to matriculate means to attend school; and celibacy means not being married.) Taking advantage of large numbers of voters with low education levels, Smathers beat Pepper.

Today, candidates frequently rely on attack ads to make much more controversial statements, often including those sponsored by independent groups. Although many members of Congress expressed their disgust with anonymous television ads attacking their character and politics, many supporters believe that political pressure is a necessary part of the political process.

To many civil libertarians, the restrictions on attack ads are a blatant violation of the First Amendment's guarantee of freedom of speech. Together with free airtime for political candidates, such government control of the airwaves reminds civil libertarians of oppressive dictatorships, such as the ones in Iraq under Saddam Hussein, in Nazi Germany, or in the former Soviet Union, where political dissent was silenced. Some have gone as far as to compare efforts to regulate campaign advertisements and media coverage to George Orwell's *1984*, in which two-way televisions monitor people's every move and the Thought Police suppress any dissenting thoughts.

While not everyone takes such a drastic view of restrictions on issue ads or proposals to provide free airtime to candidates, opposition has come from all parts of the political spectrum. Liberal-leaning groups such as the American Civil Liberties Union (ACLU) and conservative-leaning groups such as the National Rifle Association (NRA) united to challenge BCRA's prohibition of corporations and labor unions from running election ads.

In 2008, the Supreme Court ruled that circumstances exist in which applying BCRA's advertising restrictions would be unconstitutional.[1] In that case, an anti-abortion organization wanted to run advertisements critical of incumbent U.S. senators for blocking the consideration of people nominated by President George W. Bush for federal judgeships. The ads exhorted Wisconsin residents to call their senators and tell them to stop blocking the judicial process. Because an election was upcoming, however, these advertisements presumably violated federal law. In a split ruling, five justices ruled that BCRA could not constitutionally be applied to ban these advertisements.

In 2010, the Court went even further, ruling in *Citizens United v. Federal Election Commission* that BCRA's ban on corporate spending on campaign ads violated the constitutional freedom of speech. The Court ruled:

> Speech restrictions based on the identity of the speaker are all too often simply a means to control content.
>
> Quite apart from the purpose or effect of regulating content, moreover, the Government may commit a constitutional wrong when by law it identifies certain preferred speakers. By taking the right to speak from some and giving it to others, the Government deprives the disadvantaged person or class of the right to use speech to strive to establish worth, standing, and respect for the speaker's voice. The Government may not by these means deprive the public of the right and privilege to determine for itself what speech and speakers are worthy of consideration. The First Amendment protects speech and speaker, and the ideas that flow from each. . . .
>
> It is inherent in the nature of the political process that voters must be free to obtain information from diverse sources in order to determine how to cast their votes. At least before *Austin*, the Court had not allowed the exclusion of a class of speakers from the general public dialogue.
>
> We find no basis for the proposition that, in the context of political speech, the Government may impose restrictions on certain disfavored speakers. Both history and logic lead us to this conclusion.[2]

The *Citizens United* case upheld, rather than threatened, individual rights.

Many predicted that the *Citizens United* ruling would give undue influence to corporations, at the expense of ordinary citizens. The case, however, actually gave approval to a long line of civil libertarian criticisms of the ban on corporate spending on campaign ads. By limiting the voice of corporations, labor unions, and interest groups such as the NRA and the ACLU, the law had given others—especially the media—an unfair amount of influence. While ads were limited, news stories were not. In a brief challenging BCRA's constitutionality, the NRA argued that, while "a nonprofit advocacy group funded by individual membership dues cannot purchase time," media corporations can endorse candidates of their choice:

> Rupert Murdoch's News Corporation, for example, will be free to endorse or blackball candidates at will. Indeed, News Corporation will be free to produce a weekly television program such as *American Candidate*, [promoting] presidential candidates who have been selected by the News Corporation.[3]

The NRA also protested that BCRA banned ads by membership organizations, but not ads placed by wealthy individuals. In so doing, the NRA argued, BCRA stifles the voice of ordinary citizens: "[T]he aggregated wealth that the NRA accumulates corresponds with its members' support for its political ideas. If the NRA's voice is loud and reverberates through the halls of Congress, it is precisely because the organization is the *collective voice* of millions of Americans speaking in unison."[4]

Congress had garnered public support for restrictions on "attack ads" largely by creating a backlash against so-called special interest groups—such as the NRA and the ACLU—that have allegedly gained too much influence in politics. Some, however, have questioned this characterization, saying that these groups represent all parts of the political spectrum. As the Media Institute argued in a friend-of-the-court brief in a lawsuit challenging BCRA:

> Although proponents of campaign regulation argue that intervention is needed to prevent one-sided domination of political dialogue, the facts show that

citizens with political views falling on opposite ends of the ideological spectrum and from vastly different socio-economic backgrounds engage in issue advocacy. . . . [I]ndependent organizations of all stripes use the broadcast media to express their views on public policy issues, including health care, the environment, education, social security, international affairs, national defense, abortion, taxation, and gun control. . . . These groups are not homogeneous; they do not uniformly advance the same political agenda; "liberals" and "conservatives" alike sponsor issue advertisements.[5]

Law professor Lillian R. BeVier rejects the idea that issue advertisements give any group "undue influence." She writes, "There is . . . no constitutional warrant or means for calibrating what constitutes 'undue' influence. . . . We have no constitutional Goldilocks to say when the amount of influence possessed by advocates of particular positions is 'just right.'"[6] What BeVier means by her Goldilocks analogy is that the Constitution guarantees freedom of speech and does not allow the government to favor one type of speech over another.

The *Citizens United* ruling protects political dissent.

At the heart of freedom of speech is the ability to criticize the government without fearing retribution or having the government modify what is said. Ruling that an Alabama public official could not collect money from the *New York Times*, the U.S. Supreme Court noted that the United States has "a profound national commitment to the principle that debate on public issues should be uninhibited, robust, and wide-open, and that it may well include vehement, caustic, and sometimes unpleasantly sharp attacks on government and public officials."[7] In that case, *New York Times Co. v. Sullivan* (1964), an advertisement in the paper contained some minor inaccuracies regarding the official, but the Court overturned a lower court's libel award in the official's favor.

Because elected officials are frequent candidates for reelection, restrictions on campaign advertising simultaneously prevent citizens from criticizing their elected officials. Attorney

FROM THE BENCH

New York Times Co. v. Sullivan, 376 U.S. 254 (1964)

In this 1964 case, the U.S. Supreme Court ruled that the Constitution protects individuals who criticize public officials. The following in an excerpt from the Court's ruling:

The general proposition that freedom of expression upon public questions is secured by the First Amendment has long been settled by our decisions. The constitutional safeguard, we have said, "was fashioned to assure unfettered interchange of ideas for the bringing about of political and social changes desired by the people." . . . The First Amendment, said Judge Learned Hand, "presupposes that right conclusions are more likely to be gathered out of a multitude of tongues, than through any kind of authoritative selection. To many this is, and always will be, folly; but we have staked upon it our all." . . .

[There has been] a profound national commitment to the principle that debate on public issues should be uninhibited, robust, and wide-open, and that it may well include vehement, caustic, and sometimes unpleasantly sharp attacks on government and public officials. . . . The present advertisement, as an expression of grievance and protest on one of the major public issues of our time, would seem clearly to qualify for the constitutional protection. The question is whether it forfeits that protection by the falsity of some of its factual statements and by its alleged defamation of respondent. . . .

The constitutional guarantees require, we think, a federal rule that prohibits a public official from recovering damages for a defamatory falsehood relating to his official conduct unless he proves that the statement was made . . . with "actual malice"—that is, with knowledge that it was false or with reckless disregard of whether it was false or not.

Erik S. Jaffe and the Cato Institute's Robert A. Levy have argued that any federal regulation of campaign advertisements is unconstitutional. Jaffe and Levy write, "When a corporation or union expressly advocates the election or defeat of a candidate, that act—no less than issue advocacy—lies at the heart of the First Amendment."[8]

The *Citizens United* ruling upheld the requirement that the campaign advertisements identify their sponsors. Some, however, have criticized this requirement as chilling speech. Anonymous criticisms certainly have a lengthy history in American politics: for example, Benjamin Franklin frequently wrote under fictional names while criticizing Pennsylvania's colonial government, as did a number of the other Founding Fathers on a variety of issues. The ACLU has argued that requiring advertisements to disclose the source of their funding "violate longstanding First Amendment rules designed to protect anonymous political speech and the right to associate with controversial political groups."[9]

Government regulation of TV election coverage is unconstitutional and undemocratic.

After passage of BCRA, campaign reformers like Senators McCain and Feingold turned their attention to proposals to require broadcasters to give politicians free access to the broadcasts of privately owned television stations. They argued that requiring television stations to provide free airtime to candidates and carry political debates would help "clean up" politics. They introduced the Political Campaign Broadcast Activity Improvements Act, which would have required television stations—as a condition of retaining their government license—to air two hours per week of programming such as debates, interviews, or candidate statements in the weeks prior to a federal election.

Many view free airtime legislation as problematic. On the one hand, allowing free airtime to all candidates would distract people from the important issues because "fringe" candidates would detract viewers' attention from "legitimate" candidates. Critics of systems that give public support to

QUOTABLE

Justice Antonin Scalia

In the 2003 case of *McConnell v. FEC*, the majority of the U.S. Supreme Court upheld limitations on political advertising during the election season and upheld BCRA's advertising restrictions. Justice Scalia dissented:

> This is a sad day for the freedom of speech. Who could have imagined that the same Court which, within the past four years, has sternly disapproved of restrictions upon such inconsequential forms of expression as virtual child pornography, . . . tobacco advertising, . . . and sexually explicit cable programming . . . would smile with favor upon a law that cuts to the heart of what the First Amendment is meant to protect: the right to criticize the government. For that is what the most offensive provisions of this legislation are all about.
>
> We are governed by Congress, and this legislation prohibits the criticism of Members of Congress by those entities most capable of giving such criticism loud voice: national political parties and corporations, both of the commercial and the not-for-profit sort. It forbids pre-election criticism of incumbents by corporations, even not-for-profit corporations, by use of their general funds; and forbids national party use of "soft" money to fund "issue ads" that incumbents find so offensive.
>
> To be sure, the legislation is evenhanded: It similarly prohibits criticism of the candidates who oppose Members of Congress in their reelection bids. But as everyone knows, this is an area in which evenhandedness is not fairness. If all electioneering were evenhandedly prohibited, incumbents would have an enormous advantage. Likewise, if incumbents and challengers are limited to the same quantity of electioneering, incumbents are favored.

(Justice Scalia did not have to wait long to see a majority of the Court adopt his position. In the 2010 *Citizens United* case, the Court reversed itself and held that the restrictions were unconstitutional.)

Source: *McConnell v. Federal Election Commission*, 540 U.S. 93 (2003) (Scalia, J., dissenting).

candidates—such as campaign funding or free airtime—have denounced providing benefits to candidates such as: "convicted felon Lyndon LaRouche, John Hagelin of the Natural Law Party (which advocates greater use of Transcendental Meditation), and Lenora Fulani of the New Alliance Party (a socialist party that has been accused of engaging in cult-type brainwashing)."[10]

On the other hand, it would be difficult for a free airtime bill to exclude fringe candidates, because doing so would amount to government censorship of controversial viewpoints. Pete du Pont, the former governor of Delaware, criticized an earlier proposal that would have provided free airtime to "ballot-worthy candidates." He questioned, for example, whether Strom Thurmond's pro-segregation "Dixiecrat" party in 1948 would have been considered ballot-worthy.[11]

Many civil libertarians believe that it is dangerous for government to take control of private industry, even temporarily; the danger is especially significant when government takes control of the media. Edward H. Crane of the Cato Institute writes: "'Airwaves' is a misnomer. Radio and television broadcasting utilizes electromagnetic radiation, which occurs in a state of nature.... Turning [it] into communication requires a significant investment [like] turning naturally occurring iron ore into steel."[12] In Crane's opinion, the television industry is a private industry that the government should not be able to "commandeer" for campaigning purposes.

Broadcasters have also voiced strong objections to free airtime proposals because they feel that such requirements harm them financially and interfere with editorial control. Much like their opposition to restrictions on advertising, civil libertarians believe that government control of the airwaves threatens free speech, especially during critical campaign times.

Part of the objection by broadcasters to free airtime proposals is practical. Broadcast television, and to a lesser extent, cable television, relies on advertising revenue to make a profit. Political advertising is an important source of revenue, and though campaign reformers have accused broadcasters of extorting money

Excerpts from a Proposal for Free Airtime for Political Candidates

(a) In General—

(1) Program Content Requirements— [The] Federal Communications Commission may not determine that a broadcasting station has met its obligation to operate in the public interest unless the station demonstrates to the satisfaction of the Commission that—

(A) it broadcast at least 2 hours per week of candidate-centered programming or issue-centered programming during each of the 6 weeks preceding a Federal election, including at least 4 of the weeks immediately preceding a general election; and

(B) not less than 1 hour of such programming was broadcast in each of those weeks during the period beginning at 5:00 P.M. and ending at 11:35 P.M. in the time zone in which the primary broadcast audience for the station is located.

(2) Nightowl Broadcasts not Counted— For purposes of paragraph (1) any such programming broadcast between midnight and 6:00 A.M. in the time zone in which the primary broadcast audience for the station is located shall not be taken into account.

(b) DEFINITIONS— In this section . . .

(2) Candidate-Centered Programming— The term "candidate-centered programming"—

(A) includes debates, interviews, candidate statements, and other program formats that provide for a discussion of issues by the candidate; but

(B) does not include paid political advertisements. . . .

(4) Issue-Centered Programming— The term "issue-centered programming"—

(A) includes debates, interviews, statements, and other program formats that provide for a discussion of any ballot measure which appears on a ballot in a forthcoming election; but

(B) does not include paid political advertisements.

Source: Political Campaign Broadcast Activity Improvements Act, S. 3124 § 3, 107th Congress (2002).

from political candidates, broadcasters say that they certainly have not taken advantage of political candidates; in fact, broadcasters have begrudgingly complied with regulations that require television stations to give their best possible ad rates to political candidates. To require stations to give free airtime to candidates takes it a step too far.

Broadcasters argue that they already devote a significant amount of coverage to political campaigns through news stories, interviews, and debates. Free airtime proposals ignore an obvious point: Viewers are not really interested in the type of programming that campaign reformers want to impose on the public. Broadcasters are in the business of making money and therefore broadcast programming that will attract the most viewers; if people were interested in political programming, then broadcasters would carry more of it. The National Association of Broadcasters (NAB) insists that not all candidates actually want to participate in debates. A spokesperson for NAB said, "One of the constant challenges faced by broadcasters is persuading candidates to actually accept the numerous free airtime and debate offers from local stations."[13]

Summary

Civil libertarians applauded the U.S. Supreme Court's *Citizens United* ruling. Any ban on any paid political speech, including attack ads, amounts to government regulation of political speech and squelches criticism of elected officials—principles that offend the Constitution. Many are calling upon Congress to keep out of regulating television, rejecting the idea that the airwaves are a "public trust" and maintaining that government control of the media endangers democracy.

The Future of American Democracy

S ince the controversial presidential election in 2000, many American citizens have wondered whether incremental changes in our system of campaigning and voting—such as campaign finance reform efforts and the Help America Vote Act—are enough to preserve our democracy. Some people have called for radical changes to the American system of government.

One such proposal is to eliminate the Electoral College, which elects the president using representatives from each state. Although Al Gore won the "popular vote"—meaning that more people voted for him than for George W. Bush (even without counting the disputed ballots in Florida and elsewhere)—Bush won the election in more key states than Gore did, so the Electoral College chose Bush as president. Although many people believe that the system makes little sense, the Electoral College is deeply rooted in the American system of government, in which the founders wanted to ensure that states had a major voice in the federal government.

Most observers believe that it will be difficult to eliminate the Electoral College, and not simply because history is on its side. It is always difficult to change "the system," primarily because the people responsible for changing the laws—our elected officials—are the same people who have gained power through the existing system. With its bans on attack ads and limits on party fundraising, the Bipartisan Campaign Reform Act (BCRA) has been called an "incumbency protection" law because it makes it more difficult for challengers to unseat elected officials.

Despite facing resistance to change, reformers carry on with new initiatives that they hope will help not only give every person the opportunity to vote, but also make it easier to vote and make each person's vote more meaningful. One idea is to hold elections using the Internet, with the goal of increasing voter participation dramatically. Even if everyone votes, however, many votes will continue to be "wasted" in our "winner-take-all" system, in which only a plurality, sometimes not even 50 percent, of voters in any district elect the candidate of their choice.

Online Elections

One change that many people have suggested is to hold elections over the Internet; in fact, it has been tried in several places. To proponents, it makes perfect sense to use the Internet for voting. Journalist Jeffrey Birnbaum writes: "Surely if we can buy and then register a car over the Internet, we can register to vote and then actually cast a ballot. It only makes sense that we should harness the Internet in ways that will open our democracy to more and more people."[1]

The Arizona Democratic Party experimented with Internet voting during the 2000 presidential primary—this election's purpose was to choose the party's nominee for president, not to cast votes for president in the November general election, in which all registered voters can participate. It was, however, an officially sanctioned election with the option of voting online, and many hope that in the future, such opportunities will continue. The Arizona primary election demonstrated that the availability of online voting has the potential to greatly increase voter participation, especially among minority voters. According to a press release by election.com, which managed the online election:

> The results showed that the minority vote was strengthened significantly by high voter turnout, and in many cases by much more than the overall baseline increase in turnout.
>
> "I'm pleased that our efforts, in conjunction with election.com, to make this the most inclusive, accessible election ever, increased voter turnout by more than 600%," said Mark Fleisher, Chairman of the Arizona Democratic Party. "In comparison to both 1992 and 1996, voter turnout increased significantly in nearly all counties and legislative districts. . . ."
>
> Overall, voter turnout was up 622% over 1996. In the largely Hispanic legislative districts 22 and 23 in Maricopa county, turnout increased by 828% and 1011% respectively. In Apache county, turnout increased by 515% compared to 1996.[2]

Online voting has strong critics, however. In the decade since Arizona's experiment, states have been slow to adopt the practice. As of early 2010, just 16 states had adopted online voting, according to the *New York Times*, and the paper's editorial board argued that it was still not a reliable means of running an election. The editorial argued:

> E-mail can be intercepted, and voting Web sites can be hacked or taken down by malicious attacks. There are not even agreed-upon standards for what safety measures are necessary. . . .

The Internet … can be a good way to get information about elections and candidates out to faraway voters, and to deliver blank ballots. Right now, those ballots should not be returned online.[3]

THE LETTER OF THE LAW

Twelfth Amendment to the United States Constitution (1804)

After problems with the original Electoral College procedure (outlined in Article II, Section 1, Clause 3 of the U.S. Constitution), arose during the presidential elections of 1796 and 1800, the Twelfth Amendment provided a new procedure by which the president and vice president are elected:

> The Electors shall meet in their respective states and vote by ballot for President and Vice-President, one of whom, at least, shall not be an inhabitant of the same state with themselves; they shall name in their ballots the person voted for as President, and in distinct ballots the person voted for as Vice-President, and they shall make distinct lists of all persons voted for as President, and of all persons voted for as Vice-President, and of the number of votes for each, which lists they shall sign and certify, and transmit sealed to the seat of the government of the United States, directed to the President of the Senate.
>
> The President of the Senate shall, in the presence of the Senate and House of Representatives, open all the certificates and the votes shall then be counted.
>
> The person having the greatest number of votes for President, shall be the President, if such number be a majority of the whole number of Electors appointed; and if no person have such majority, then from the persons having the highest numbers not exceeding three on the list of those voted for as President, the House of Representatives shall choose immediately, by ballot, the President. But in choosing the President, the votes shall be taken by states, the representation from each state having one vote; a quorum for this purpose shall consist of a member or members from two-thirds of the states, and a majority of all the states shall be necessary to a choice.

Source: U.S. Constitution, Amendment XII (1804).

THE GERRY-MANDER.

The term *gerrymandering* comes from the name of Elbridge Gerry, who served as governor of Massachusetts from 1810 to 1812. During his time in office, Gerry drew a bizarre-looking congressional district *(seen here)* to benefit his political party that some people believed look like either a salamander or a monster.

It might be years—if ever—before the nation is ready for online general elections. One of the biggest concerns is voter fraud. Arizona required voters to input seven-digit identification numbers that were mailed to registered Democrats before the election. There was, however, no good way to verify that the person entering the identification number was the person to whom it was assigned. Compared to systems in which voters must appear in person and sign a log, the anonymity of Internet voting has even greater potential for fraud. Additionally, some people have expressed concern with electronic voting systems that do not maintain a "hard copy" of the votes: If a candidate wanted to challenge the election, there would be no way of doing a recount.

The Politics of Redistricting

Another problem with the current system, in which states are divided into districts that each elect one candidate, is that the district lines are subject to manipulation. Congressional districts change regularly for two reasons: changes in the number of representatives for a particular state and population shifts within a state. Someone has to draw the new district lines, and that responsibility usually falls to the majority party, which can draw the districts in a way that favors the party. By maximizing the number of districts in which it has a majority, the party can maximize the number of representatives. Redistricting in a way that gives one party an advantage is commonly known as "gerrymandering," a term that comes from the name of former Massachusetts governor Elbridge Gerry: The state had an oddly shaped district that looked like a salamander.

Political science professor Douglas J. Amy explains that there are two techniques for gerrymandering: "cracking" and "packing."[4] Cracking involves splitting a district in which a majority of voters support the other party and relocating voters to districts in which they are the political minority. Packing involves putting as many of the other party's voters as possible into as few districts as possible. Whether the other party controls 51 percent of the votes in a district or 100 percent of the votes in that district, it still only gets one representative. Therefore, packing voters into districts means that the same number of voters elects fewer representatives in Congress.

Though "gerrymandering" has traditionally been a tool for a majority party to increase its dominance, some have applied the term to efforts to increase the voting power of racial minorities. For a time, in response to rulings by the U.S. Department of Justice, states created congressional districts comprising a majority of African-American voters. For example, when Georgia gained an eleventh congressional district after the 1990 census, the Department of Justice insisted that three of the districts be majority African American, reflecting the fact that 27 percent of Georgia's population was African American. Because the state already had two majority-African-American districts, the state legislature created a congressional district that included predominantly African-American sections of Atlanta and Savannah— two cities more than 250 miles (402 kilometers) apart—as well as the area in between.

The Supreme Court invalidated the district, however, in a ruling that put strict limits on the ability of states to take race into account when creating legislative districts. In *Miller v. Johnson*, the Court held:

> The [trial] court found it was "exceedingly obvious" from the shape of the Eleventh District, together with the relevant racial demographics, that the drawing of narrow land bridges to incorporate within the District outlying appendages containing nearly 80 percent of the district's total black population was a deliberate attempt to bring black populations into the district. . . . Although by comparison with other districts the geometric shape of the Eleventh District may not seem bizarre on its face, when its shape is considered in conjunction with its racial and population densities, the story of racial gerrymandering seen by the District Court becomes much clearer. The [trial] court had before it considerable additional evidence showing that the General Assembly was motivated by a predominant, overriding desire to assign black populations to the Eleventh District. . . .

Only if our political system and our society cleanse themselves of that discrimination will all members of the polity share an equal opportunity to gain public office regardless of race.... The end is neither assured nor well served, however, by carving electorates into racial blocs.... It takes a shortsighted and unauthorized view of the Voting Rights Act to invoke that statute, which has played a decisive role in redressing some of our worst forms of discrimination, to demand the very racial stereotyping the Fourteenth Amendment forbids.[5]

The Court's decision was widely criticized. In dissenting from the majority's decision, Justice John Paul Stevens wrote:

[It is distressing that the Court equates] traditional gerrymanders, designed to maintain or enhance a dominant group's power, with a dominant group's decision to share its power with a previously underrepresented group. In my view, districting plans violate the Equal Protection Clause when they "serve no purpose other than to favor one segment—whether racial, ethnic, religious, economic, or political—that may occupy a position of strength at a particular point in time, or to disadvantage a politically weak segment of the community."... In contrast, I do not see how a districting plan that favors a politically weak group can violate equal protection....

The Court's refusal to distinguish an enactment that helps a minority group from enactments that cause it harm is especially unfortunate at the intersection of race and voting, given that African Americans and other disadvantaged groups have struggled so long and so hard for inclusion in that most central exercise of our democracy.[6]

In an unusual, highly technical case a few years later, the Supreme Court held that federal law did not require the creation of voting districts in which minorities represent a near-majority, and specifically, that North Carolina was not required to split counties in order to form a 40 percent African-American district, though the state could have done so if permitted by state law.[7] The Court sided against the state, with some justices reasoning that, although federal law would have allowed the creation of a geographically compact majority-African-American district, the creation of a district with 40 percent minority representation did not justify ignoring state law.

The Effect of Elections on Racial and Political Minorities.

As the example of the 2000 presidential election demonstrates, nowhere is the phrase "winner-take-all" more appropriate than in American politics. In a national election for president, one candidate wins. The same is true of statewide elections for seats in the U.S. Senate and for district elections to the House of Representatives.

Some people have begun to wonder if winner-take-all is the right way to elect representatives to Congress. Most states—except for the least populous states, such as North and South Dakota—elect more than one representative. Under the current system, each state electing multiple representatives is divided into congressional districts, each of which elects one representative. In each district, one person wins and everyone else loses. Even with a great deal of support statewide, a candidate must win his or her district in order to be elected. Additionally, in a state that is, for example, 40 percent Republican, there is no guarantee that 40 percent of the state's representatives will be Republican, because any successful candidate must win a plurality of the vote in his or her district.

Under the current winner-take-all system, it is difficult for racial minorities and minority political parties to gain a share of political power. To remedy this perceived unfairness, some people have called for abandoning the current system in favor of "proportional representation." Under such a system, the state's voters would not be divided into single-representative districts, but instead each district (or the entire state) would elect multiple representatives. Professor Douglas J. Amy recommends that each district elect at least five seats.[8] In a five-candidate district, the top five candidates would win; therefore a candidate would only need to attract roughly 20 percent of the vote to ensure victory. With proportional representation, minority groups could more easily elect a candidate of their choice. Although common in Europe, proportional representation would mark a significant change from current American politics.

The state of California has adopted proportional representation in a limited way. There, voters approved of a measure that would require proportional voting in places where minority voters appear to have been shut out of the political process by winner-take-all elections. Backed by the voting rights organizations FairVote and Common Cause, Latino voters challenged local election procedures used by the city of Modesto. Because the entire population of the city elected each seat on the city council, a minority candidate would have had to win a majority of white votes to gain any seat. As the organizations explained in a legal brief:

> Although the population of Modesto, California, is fully 25.6 percent Latino, there are no Latinos on the Modesto City Council, and only one Latino has ever been elected to the council in its 94-year history. These facts are strong indicators of minority vote dilution in Modesto. They indicate that the winner-take-all, at-large voting system used in Modesto City Council elections usually enables bloc voting majority voters to prevent an identifiable subgroup of the population (i.e., Latinos) from electing candidates of their choice or

influencing the outcome of elections. Such an extended history of electoral futility strongly suggests that voting strength in Modesto has not simply been diminished by winner-take-all, at-large elections. It has been eliminated entirely.[9]

After a California appeals court rejected the city's challenge to the constitutionality of the law and the U.S. Supreme Court refused to hear the city's appeal,[10] the city changed its election procedures, with the November 2009 elections featuring for the first time the selection of city council members by geographic district—and new opportunities for Latino candidates.

Summary

Since the 2000 presidential election, in which many people either could not vote or had their ballots discarded, Congress has enacted significant legislation reforming the electoral process. Many people, however, think that further reforms are needed to ensure each citizen a voice in politics. Some have suggested that Internet elections could increase the number of people who vote, but critics worry about fraud. A long-term solution might be a system of proportional representation that would give more of a voice to political and racial minorities.

Beginning Legal Research

The goals of each book in the POINT/COUNTERPOINT series are not only to give the reader a basic introduction to a controversial issue affecting society, but also to encourage the reader to explore the issue more fully. This Appendix is meant to serve as a guide to the reader in researching the current state of the law as well as exploring some of the public policy arguments as to why existing laws should be changed or new laws are needed.

Although some sources of law can be found primarily in law libraries, legal research has become much faster and more accessible with the advent of the Internet. This Appendix discusses some of the best starting points for free access to laws and court decisions, but surfing the Web will uncover endless additional sources of information. Before you can research the law, however, you must have a basic understanding of the American legal system.

The most important source of law in the United States is the Constitution. Originally enacted in 1787, the Constitution outlines the structure of our federal government, as well as setting limits on the types of laws that the federal government and state governments can enact. Through the centuries, a number of amendments have added to or changed the Constitution, most notably the first 10 amendments, which collectively are known as the "Bill of Rights" and which guarantee important civil liberties.

Reading the plain text of the Constitution provides little information. For example, the Constitution prohibits "unreasonable searches and seizures" by the police. To understand concepts in the Constitution, it is necessary to look to the decisions of the U.S. Supreme Court, which has the ultimate authority in interpreting the meaning of the Constitution. For example, the U.S. Supreme Court's 2001 decision in *Kyllo v. United States* held that scanning the outside of a person's house using a heat sensor to determine whether the person is growing marijuana is an unreasonable search—if it is done without first getting a search warrant from a judge. Each state also has its own constitution and a supreme court that is the ultimate authority on its meaning.

Also important are the written laws, or "statutes," passed by the U.S. Congress and the individual state legislatures. As with constitutional provisions, the U.S. Supreme Court and the state supreme courts are the ultimate authorities in interpreting the meaning of federal and state laws, respectively. However, the U.S. Supreme Court might find that a state law violates the U.S. Constitution, and a state supreme court might find that a state law violates either the state or U.S. Constitution.

Not every controversy reaches either the U.S. Supreme Court or the state supreme courts, however. Therefore, the decisions of other courts are also important. Trial courts hear evidence from both sides and make a decision, while appeals courts review the decisions made by trial courts. Sometimes rulings from appeals courts are appealed further to the U.S. Supreme Court or the state supreme courts.

Lawyers and courts refer to statutes and court decisions through a formal system of citations. Use of these citations reveals which court made the decision or which legislature passed the statute, and allows one to quickly locate the statute or court case online or in a law library. For example, the Supreme Court case *Brown v. Board of Education* has the legal citation 347 U.S. 483 (1954). At a law library, this 1954 decision can be found on page 483 of volume 347 of the U.S. Reports, which are the official collection of the Supreme Court's decisions. On the following page, you will find samples of all the major kinds of legal citation.

Finding sources of legal information on the Internet is relatively simple thanks to "portal" sites such as findlaw.com and lexisone.com, which allow the user to access a variety of constitutions, statutes, court opinions, law review articles, news articles, and other useful sources of information. For example, findlaw.com offers access to all Supreme Court decisions since 1893. Other useful sources of information include gpo.gov, which contains a complete copy of the U.S. Code, and thomas.loc.gov, which offers access to bills pending before Congress, as well as recently passed laws. Of course, the Internet changes every second of every day, so it is best to do some independent searching.

Of course, many people still do their research at law libraries, some of which are open to the public. For example, some state governments and universities offer the public access to their law collections. Law librarians can be of great assistance, as even experienced attorneys need help with legal research from time to time.

Common Citation Forms

Source of Law	Sample Citation	Notes
U.S. Supreme Court	*Employment Division v. Smith*, 485 U.S. 660 (1988)	The U.S. Reports is the official record of Supreme Court decisions. There is also an unofficial Supreme Court ("S. Ct.") reporter.
U.S. Court of Appeals	*United States v. Lambert*, 695 F.2d 536 (11th Cir.1983)	Appellate cases appear in the Federal Reporter, designated by "F." The 11th Circuit has jurisdiction in Alabama, Florida, and Georgia.
U.S. District Court	*Carillon Importers, Ltd. v. Frank Pesce Group, Inc.*, 913 F.Supp. 1559 (S.D.Fla.1996)	Federal trial-level decisions are reported in the Federal Supplement ("F. Supp."). Some states have multiple federal districts; this case originated in the Southern District of Florida.
U.S. Code	Thomas Jefferson Commemoration Commission Act, 36 U.S.C., §149 (2002)	Sometimes the popular names of legislation—names with which the public may be familiar—are included with the U.S. Code citation.
State Supreme Court	*Sterling v. Cupp*, 290 Ore. 611, 614, 625 P.2d 123, 126 (1981)	The Oregon Supreme Court decision is reported in both the state's reporter and the Pacific regional reporter.
State Statute	Pennsylvania Abortion Control Act of 1982, 18 Pa. Cons. Stat. 3203-3220 (1990)	States use many different citation formats for their statutes.

Cases and Statutes

New York Times Co. v. Sullivan, 376 U.S. 254 (1964)

Held that a public official cannot collect libel damages for inaccurate statements without demonstrating "actual malice."

Red Lion Broadcasting Co. v. FCC, 395 U.S. 367 (1969)

Held that the government can require broadcasters to act in the public interest because they use the public airwaves.

Voting Rights Act, 42 U.S.C. § 1973

Outlaws tactics used to disenfranchise minority voters, such as poll taxes, literacy tests, and character tests. Also requires cities, counties, and states to obtain pre-clearance from the federal government before changing election procedures or districts.

National Voter Registration Act, 42 U.S.C. §§ 1973gg

Commonly called the "Motor Voter" law; requires states to provide voter registration opportunities at motor vehicle bureaus and other public offices.

Buckley v. Valeo, 424 U.S. 1 (1976) (per curiam)

Held that the government can regulate campaign contributions more closely than it can regulate other forms of political expression.

Austin v. Michigan Chamber of Commerce, 494 U.S. 652 (1990)

Upheld state law banning campaign expenditures by corporations. The Court overruled *Austin* in the 2010 case *Citizens United v. Federal Election Commission.*

Miller v. Johnson, 515 U.S. 900 (1995)

Struck down an oddly shaped legislative district in Georgia created with the specific purpose of having African Americans constitute a majority of voters.

Nixon v. Shrink Missouri Government PAC, 528 U.S. 377 (2000)

Upheld Missouri's limit on campaign contributions.

Bush v. Gore, 531 U.S. 98 (2000) (per curiam)

Ended Florida's recount of ballots in the 2000 presidential election.

Bipartisan Campaign Reform Act (BCRA), Pub. L. No. 107-155 (March 22, 2002)

Outlawed "soft money" contributions to political parties; placed stricter limits on campaign advertising.

Help America Vote Act, 42 U.S.C. § 15483 (2002)

Mandated "provisional balloting," so that nobody is turned away from the polls; imposed identification requirements for voting.

McConnell v. Federal Election Commission, 540 U.S. 93 (2003)

Upheld most of BCRA's provisions. Overruled in part in 2010, with the Court holding in *Citizens United v. Federal Election Commission* that limits on corporate spending on campaign advertisements are unconstitutional.

Randall v. Sorrell, 438 U.S. 230 (2006)
> Struck down a state law limiting individual and political party contributions to candidates for state office to between $200 and $400. The justices split on their rationale, with some saying any limits were unconstitutional and others saying the amounts were too restrictive.

Federal Election Commission v. Wisconsin Right to Life, 546 U.S. 410 (2007)
> Limited BCRA's ban on issue advertisements during election season to ads that clearly have no other purpose than to influence elections.

Crawford v. Marion County Election Board, 128 S.Ct. 1610 (2008)
> Upheld Indiana's voter identification law.

Bartlett v. Strickland, 556 U.S. 1 (2009)
> Held that federal law neither required nor prohibited the creation of voting districts in which racial minorities made up a near majority of eligible voters.

Northwest Austin Municipal Utility District No. 1 v. Holder, No. 08-322 (June 22, 2009)
> Held that any political subdivision holding elections may seek exemption from the Voting Rights Act's federal preclearance requirements for changing election procedures.

Citizens United v. Federal Election Commission, No. 08-205 (January 21, 2010)
> Reversed *Austin* and parts of *McConnell*, holding that bans on corporate and union expenditures on election ads violate their free speech rights.

Terms and Concepts

Attack ads	Issue-centered programming
Bribery	Partisan politics
Broadcast spectrum	Political parties
Campaign contributions	Poll tax
Campaign finance reform	Preclearance
Candidate-centered programming	Proportional representation
Civil disobedience	Provisional balloting
Corruption	Public interest
Discrimination	Sham issue ads
Disenfranchisement	Soft money
Disproportionate effect	Voter error
Electoral College	Voter fraud
Free airtime	Voting rights
Free speech	Winner-take-all
Intent of the voter	

NOTES ||||▷

Introduction: Voting: The Cornerstone of Democracy?

1 U.S. Census Bureau, press release, "Voter Turnout Increases by 5 Million in 2008 Presidential Election" (July 20, 2009).

2 U.S. Commission on Civil Rights, *Voting Irregularities in Florida During the 2000 Presidential Election* (Aug. 2002). http://www.usccr.gov/.

3 Ibid.

4 *Bush v. Gore,* 531 U.S. 98 (2000) (per curiam).

5 Neal Peirce, "Taming 'Winner Take All'—a Cure for All Elections Malaise," Stateline.org (Sept. 18, 2002).

Point: Voting Rights Require Strong Protections

1 Memorandum from A. Rosen to Mr. Belmont (Sept. 18, 1964). Part of the FBI's online FOIA reading room. http://foia.fbi.gov.

2 42 U.S.C. § 1973 (2000).

3 42 U.S.C. § 1973-gg (2000).

4 Pub. L. No. 107-252, 116 Stat. 1666 (2002).

5 Eric Lipton and Ian Urbina, "In 5-Year Effort, Scant Evidence of Voter Fraud," *New York Times* (April 12, 2007). http://www.nytimes.com/2007/04/12/washington/12fraud.html.

6 U.S. Commission on Civil Rights, *Voting Irregularities in Florida During the 2000 Presidential Election.*

7 Ibid.

8 Cong. Rec. E220 (Feb. 27, 2001).

9 *Crawford v. Marion County Election Bd.,* 128 S.Ct. 1610 (2008) (Souter, J. dissenting), p. 4.

10 Cong. Rec. E220 (Feb. 27, 2001).

11 Brief for NAACP Legal Defense Fund, *Northwest Austin Municipal Utility District No. 1 v. Holder,* No. 08-322 (June 22, 2009), p. 13.

12 Ibid.

13 Ibid., p. 14.

14 U.S. Commission on Civil Rights, *Voting Irregularities in Florida During the 2000 Presidential Election.*

15 Cong. Rec. S 1228 (Feb. 27, 2002).

16 National Council of La Raza, press release, "NCLR Urges Congress to Vote No on the Help America Vote Act" (Oct. 9, 2002).

Counterpoint: Strict Registration Requirements Prevent Fraud

1 Kathleen Wereszynski, "Stunt Reveals Holes in 'Motor Voter' Law," Foxnews.com (June 17, 2001).

2 Jonah Goldberg, "Vote.con: The Perils of 'Cyber-Democracy," *National Review* (Dec. 20, 1999).

3 Michelle Malkin, "The Pro-Barack Vote-Fraud Drive," *New York Post* (Oct. 8, 2008).

4 Byron York, "Bad Lands, Bad Votes," *National Review* (Dec. 19, 2002).

5 Ibid.

6 Jim Boulet Jr., "Will Noncitizens Decide the Election?" *National Review* (Nov. 10, 2000).

7 U.S. Commission on Civil Rights, *Voting Irregularities in Florida During the 2000 Presidential Election* (Dissenting Statement by Commissioners Thernstrom and Redenbaugh).

8 Ibid.

9 Brief for Pacific Legal Foundation, *Northwest Austin Municipal Utility District No. 1 v. Holder,* No. 08-322 (June 22, 2009), p. 19.

10 Michelle Malkin, "The Pro-Barack Vote Fraud Drive."

11 Cong. Rec. S1224 (Feb. 27, 2002).

12 *Hearings on the Motor Voter Act and Voter Fraud Before the Committee of Rules and Administration of the Senate,* 107th Cong. (2001) (statement of John Samples).

13 Ibid.

14 Ibid.

15 Cong. Rec. S1224 (Feb. 27, 2002).

16 Robert Pear, "Bush Signs Law Intended to End Disputes," *New York Times* (Oct. 29, 2002).

17 Ibid.

Point: Money Corrupts American Democracy

1 Kathleen Murphy, "Govs' Races Break the Bank," Stateline.org (Nov. 11, 2002).

2 Pub. L. No. 107-155 § 307 (March 27, 2002) (amending limit to $2,000); 2 U.S.C. § 441a (2000) (setting limit at $1,000).

3 Pub. L. No. 107-155 § 307 (March 27, 2002) (extending ban to cover political parties) (2 U.S.C. § 441b (2000) (banning most contributions by corporations and labor unions).

4 Russell D. Feingold, "Representative Democracy Versus Corporate Democracy: How Soft Money Erodes the Principle of 'One Person, One Vote,'" in Annelise Anderson, ed., *Political Money: Deregulating American Politics.* Stanford, Calif.: Hoover Institution Press, 2000, p. 317.

5 147 Cong. Rec. S2434 (March 19, 2001).

6 Brief for Committee for Economic Development, *McConnell v. FEC* (Dist. D.C.) (No. 02-0582).

7 Ibid.

8 147 Cong. Rec. S2434 (March 19, 2001).

9 Brief for Committee for Economic Development, *McConnell v. FEC* (Dist. D.C.) (No. 02-0582).

10 *McConnell v. Federal Election Commission*, 540 U.S. 93 (opinion of Stevens and O'Connor, JJ.), p. 37.

11 Ibid., p. 38.

12 *McConnell v. Federal Election Commission*, 540 U.S. 93 (2003).

13 *Citizens United v. Federal Election Commission*, No. 08-205 (Jan. 21, 2010).

14 Jay Reeves, "N.Y. Dollars Key in District 7 Race," *Montgomery Advertiser* (June 27, 2002).

15 Jonathan Rosenblum, "Payback Time for New York Jews," *Hamodia* (Sept. 6, 2002). http://www.jewishmediaresources.com.

16 Thomas B. Edsall, "Impact of McKinney Loss Worries Some Democrats: Tension Between Blacks, Jews a Concern," *Washington Post* (Aug. 22, 2002), p. A4.

17 Brief for Former Leaders of ACLU, *McConnell v. FEC* (Dist. D.C.) (No. 02-0582).

18 *Randall v. Sorrell*, 438 U.S. 230 (2006).

19 Ibid. (Souter, J., dissenting), pp. 5–6.

20 Ibid., p. 6.

Counterpoint: Campaign Contributions Are Political Speech

1 Tom Bethell, "The Money Chase," in Annelise Anderson, ed., *Political Money: Deregulating American Politics*, p. 251.

2 Ibid.

3 Doug Bandow, "Best Reform Is No Limits," *USA Today* (Aug. 11, 2000).

4 Steven E. Schier, "One Cheer for Soft Money," in Christopher Luna, ed., *Campaign Finance Reform.* New York: H.W. Wilson Company, 2001, pp. 90, 92.

5 Ibid., pp. 91, 93.

6 Russell D. Feingold, "Representative Democracy Versus Corporate Democracy: How Soft Money Erodes the Principle of 'One Person, One Vote,'" in Annelise Anderson, ed., *Political Money: Deregulating American Politics*, p. 317.

7 Allison R. Hayward, "'Conservative' Campaign-Finance Reform?" *National Review* (Sept. 14, 2000).

8 John Samples, "'Soft Money' Aids Democracy," *USA Today* (Sept. 29, 2000).

9 Ibid.

10 Doug Bandow, "Best Reform Is No Limits."

11 Tom Bethell, "The Money Chase," in Annelise Anderson, ed., *Political Money: Deregulating American Politics*, p. 251.

12 *Randall v. Sorrell*, 438 U.S. 230 (2006) (Opinion of Scalia, J.), p. 6.

13 Michael Barone, "Lessons from Rep. Cynthia McKinney's Defeat," *U.S. News & World Report* (Aug. 29, 2002).

14 *Randall v. Sorrell*, 438 U.S. 230 (2006) (Thomas, J., concurring in the judgment), p. 8.

15 *Randall v. Sorrell*, 438 U.S. 230 (2006) (Opinion of Scalia, J.), p. 6.

16 Erik S. Jaffe and Robert A. Levy, "Real Campaign Reform," *Regulation*, Fall 2002, p. 8.

17 Brief for Institute for Justice and Cato Institute, *McConnell v. FEC* (Dist. D.C.) (No. 02-0582).

Point: Regulating Television Promotes Fair Campaigns

1 Darrell M. West, *Checkbook Democracy: How Money Corrupts Political Campaigns,* Boston: Northeastern University Press, 2000, p. 30.

2 Mike Denison, "Taylor Quits Senate Race," *Great Falls Tribune* (Oct. 11, 2002).

3 Ibid.

4 424 U.S. 1 (1976) (per curiam).

5 Brief for Former Leaders of ACLU, *McConnell v. FEC* (Dist. D.C.) (No. 02-0582).

6 Ibid.

7 Bipartisan Campaign Reform Act, Pub. L. No. 107-155 (March 22, 2002).

8 *Federal Election Commission v. Wisconsin Right to Life*, 546 U.S. 410 (2007), pp. 4–5.

9 *Federal Election Commission v. Wisconsin Right to Life*, 546 U.S. 410 (2007) (Souter, J., dissenting), p. 34.

10 *Citizens United v. Federal Election Comm'n*, No. 08-205 (Jan. 21, 2010).

11 Cong. Rec. S10585 (Oct. 16, 2002).

12 Jeffrey H. Birnbaum, *The Money Men: The Real Story of Fund-raising's Influence on Political Power in America.* New York: Crown Publishers, 2000, pp. 261–262.

13 Ibid., p. 262.

14 Cong. Rec. S10585-86 (Oct. 16, 2002).

15 Cong. Rec. S 10583 (Oct. 16, 2002).

16 Cong. Rec. S 10585 (Oct. 16, 2002).

17 Cong. Rec. S 10583 (Oct. 16, 2002).

18 Ric Bainter and Paul Lhevine, "Political Reform Comes from Communities," in Christopher Luna, ed., *Campaign Finance Reform*, p. 167.

Counterpoint: Regulating Television Is Unconstitutional and Undemocratic

1 *Federal Election Commission v. Wisconsin Right to Life*, 546 U.S. 410 (2007).

2 *Citizens United v. Federal Election Comm'n.* No. 08-205 (Jan. 21, 2010), pp. 24-25.

3 Brief for National Rifle Association, *McConnell v. FEC* (Dist. D.C.) (No. 02 0582).

4 Ibid.

5 Brief for Media Institute, *McConnell v. FEC* (Dist. D.C.) (No. 02-0582).

6 Lillian R. BeVier, *Campaign Finance "Reform" Proposals: A First Amendment Analysis, Cato Policy Analysis No. 282* (Cato Institute, Washington, D.C.: 1997).

7 *New York Times Co. v. Sullivan*, 376 U.S. 254 (1964).

8 Erik S. Jaffe and Robert A. Levy, "Real Campaign Reform," *Regulation* (Fall 2002).

9 Brief for ACLU, *McConnell v. FEC* (Dist. D.C.) (No. 02-0582).

10 Bradley A. Smith, *Unfree Speech: The Folly of Campaign Finance Reform.* Princeton, N.J.: Princeton University Press, 2001, p. 96.

11 Pete du Pont, "Price Controls on Democracy," in Annelise Anderson, ed., *Political Money: Degregulating American Politics*, p. 280.

12 Edward H. Crane, "The Case Against Free Radio and Television Time for Politicians," *Cato Daily News* (Feb. 20, 1996).

13 Reporters Committee for Freedom of the Press, "Campaign Reform Threatens Broadcasters' Rights," *News Media and the Law* 26 No. 3 (Summer 2002).

Conclusion: The Future of American Democracy

1 Jeffrey H. Birnbaum, *The Money Men*, p. 270.

2 Election.com, press release, (Mar. 24, 2000).

3 "Internet Voting, Still in Beta," *New York Times*, Jan. 28, 2010, http://www.nytimes.com/2010/01/28/opinion/28thu4.html.

4 Douglas J. Amy, *Real Choices/New Voices: How Proportional Representation Could Revitalize American Democracy.* New York: Columbia University Press, 1995.

5 *Miller v. Johnson*, 515 U.S. 900 (1995).

6 *Miller v. Johnson*, 515 U.S. 900 (1995) (Stevens, J, dissenting).

7 *Bartlett v. Strickland*, 556 U.S. 1 (2009).

8 Douglas J. Amy, *Real Choices/New Voices.*

9 Brief of California Common Cause and FairVote, *Sanchez v. City of Modesto*, No. F048277 (Ca. Ct. App., 5th Dist., Dec. 6, 2006).

10 *City of Modesto v. Sanchez*, No. 07-88, cert. denied (Oct. 15, 2007).

Books

Amy, Douglas J. *Real Choices/New Voices: How Proportional Representation Could Revitalize American Democracy.* New York: Columbia University Press, 1995.

Anderson, Annelise, ed. *Political Money: Deregulating American Politics.* Stanford, Calif.: Hoover Institution Press, 2000.

Birnbaum, Jeffrey H. *The Money Men: The Real Story of Fund-raising's Influence on Political Power in America.* New York: Crown Publishers, 2000.

Cohen, Joshua, and Joel Rogers, eds. *Money and Politics: Financing Our Elections Democratically.* Boston: Beacon Press, 1999.

Luna, Christopher, ed. *Campaign Finance Reform.* New York: H.W. Wilson Company, 2001.

Palazzolo, Daniel J., and James W. Caesar, eds. *Election Reform: Politics and Policy.* Lanham, Md.: Lexington Books, 2005.

Smith, Bradley A. *Unfree Speech: The Folly of Campaign Finance Reform.* Princeton, N.J.: Princeton University Press, 2001.

Utter, Glenn H., and Ruth Ann Strickland. *Campaign and Election Reform: A Reference Handbook*, Second Edition. Santa Barbara, Calif.: ABC-CLIO, 2008.

West, Darrell M. *Checkbook Democracy: How Money Corrupts Political Campaigns.* Boston: Northeastern University Press, 2000.

Web Sites

The Campaign Legal Center

http://www.camlc.org
Nonprofit legal group representing the "public interest" in campaign finance and media law cases. Extensive information about ongoing litigation is available on this Web site.

Cato Institute

http://www.cato.org
Libertarian "think tank" opposing unnecessary government regulations. Extensive information about arguments against campaign reforms and media regulations may be found here.

Center for Responsive Politics

http://www.opensecrets.org

Divulges sources of campaign financing, with analysis of controversial contributions, such as those by Enron.

The Center for Voting and Democracy

http://www.fairvote.org

In-depth information about proportional representation, redistricting, and instant-runoff voting.

Common Cause

http://www.commoncause.org

National membership organization dedicated to increasing accountability of elected officials and reducing the impact of money on politics.

Democracy 21

http://www.democracy21.org

Nonprofit organization seeking to reduce the influence of money on politics.

Election Law Blog

http://electionlawblog.org

A law professor's review of current legal controversies regarding campaign finance, election oversight, and voter access, among other issues.

Federal Election Commission

http://www.fec.gov

Federal agency overseeing campaigns and elections. Text of federal election laws and regulations and information about candidates' sources of funding may be found here.

League of Women Voters

http://www.lwv.org

National membership organization devoted to increasing citizen participation in politics. Extensive information about election and campaign finance reform is available on this Web site.

The Media Institute

http://www.mediainstitute.org

Nonprofit organization specializing in First Amendment issues that provides arguments against government regulation of advertising and broadcasting.

NAACP Legal Defense and Educational Fund

http://www.naacpldf.org

Public interest law firm representing the interests of minorities in voter access and other legal matters.

National Association of Broadcasters

http://www.nab.org
Association of radio and television broadcasters that opposes restrictions on broadcasters.

Pacific Legal Foundation

http://www.pacificlegal.org
Conservative law firm that has represented parties challenging contribution limits, federal intervention, and other restrictions on campaigning and elections.

Wiley Rein Election Law Newsletter

http://www.wileyrein.com/publications.cfm?sp=newsletters&id=8
Newsletter published by a private law firm with a group of attorneys specializing in election law.

PAGE

15: AP Images
19: AP Images
29: AP Images

47: Newscom
62: AP Images
96: Bettmann/Corbis

Page numbers in *italics* indicate photos or illustrations.

A

abortion 82
access, selling of 51
ACLU (American Civil
   Liberties Union) 53–
   55, 72–73, 82, 84
ACORN (Association of
   Community Orga-
   nizations for Reform
   Now) 36, 40–41
advertisements. *See* Tele-
   vision
airtime, free 76–80,
   87–91
Alabama 52
Alaska 42
Alito, Samuel 65
Amy, Douglas J. 97, 101
anonymity 87
Arizona 93–94
Assman, Ed 37
Association of Commu-
   nity Organizations
   for Reform Now. *See*
   ACORN
attack ads. *See* Television
*Austin Municipal Util-
   ity District No. 1 v.
   Holder* 28–30, 40

B

bailouts 28–30, 40
Bainter, Ric 78
ballots 14–17, *15*, 23, 26
Bandow, Doug 59, 63
Barone, Michael 64
Baucus, Max 70–71
BCRA (Bipartisan Cam-
   paign Reform Act)
   campaign
      advertisements and
      73–74, 75
   freedom of speech and
      53–56, 64–68
   as incumbency
      protection law 93

individual contributions
   and 51–52
McConnell v. FEC and
   64, 66, 73, 88
overview of 57
passage of 46, *47*
soft money and 47–50
as unconstitutional
   82–85
Bethell, Tom 58–59, 63
BeVier, Lillian R. 85
Biden, Joe 11
Bipartisan Campaign
   Reform Act. *See*
   BCRA
Birnbaum, Jeffrey H. 76
Bond, Christopher 41,
   43, 44
Boulet, Jim Jr. 37
bounty hunters 37
brainwashing 89
Breyer, Stephen 65
bribery, soft money vs.
   48–49
Briscoe, Mabel and Holly
   34–35, 39–40
bubble sheets 14
Buchanan, Pat *15*, 15–16
Buckley v. Valeo 46,
   53–54, 64, 66, 72
Bush, George H.W.
   69–70, 71
Bush, George W. 12–18,
   63, 82, 92
Bush, Jeb 38
Bush v. Gore 17
businesses, soft money
   and 46–50
butterfly ballots 14–16,
   15

C

California 101–102
campaign contributions
   corruption and 45–48

as essential to process
   59–63
freedom of speech and
   53–56, 64–67
from individuals 51–53,
   55–56, 63–64
soft money and 46–50
candidate-centered pro-
   gramming 90
chads, hanging and dim-
   pled 16–17
chemical manufacturers
   48–49
*Citizens United v. Federal
   Election Commission*
   46, 74, 82–87, 88
citizenship 37
Citizenship USA 37–38
civil disobedience 35
Clinton, Hillary 51–52
Clinton, William 37, 51
coercion 22–23
Coleman, Norm 18–19
commercials. *See* Television
Committee for Economic
   Development 49, 50
Common Cause 101
Congress, "winner-take-
   all" elections and
   100–102
corruption 45–48, 66
cracking 97
Crane, Edward H. 89

D

Davis, Artur 52, 64
debates, televised 76–80,
   87, 90
Democratic Party 35–39,
   43–44, 46–50, 51–52,
   55–56
dimpled chads 16–17
discrimination 21–27.
   See also Race

disenfranchisement 38, 43

dissent, protection of right to 85–87

Dodd, Christopher 44, 49

dogs 19–20, 34–35, 39–40, 41

drivers licenses 23, 28, 30–32. *See also* Motor Voter law

du Pont, Pete 89

Dukakis, Michael 69–70, 71

Dwyer, Ruth 56

E

Electoral College 12, 92–93, 95

enforcement of voting rights laws 28–32, 42–44

English First 37

Enron 49–50

environmental laws 48–49

Equal Protection Clause 99

errors 26, 38

exit polls 14

F

FairVote 101

FCC, Red Lion Broadcasting Co. v. 79

FEC (Federal Election Commission) 46, 64, 66, 73–74, 82–88

Feingold, Russ 46–47, *47*, 60, 73–78, 87

Fifteenth Amendment 21, 24–25

finance reform. *See* Campaign contributions

First Amendment. *See* Freedom of speech

Florida 12–18, 26–27, 30–32, 38–39, 81

Franken, Al 18–19

Franklin, Benjamin 87

fraud
dogs and 19–20, 34–35, 39–40, 41
efforts to register immigrants, minorities, and poor and 35–38
online elections and 96–97
redistricting and 97–100
turnout and 19–20
voting rights acts as causing widespread 39–42

free airtime 76–80, 87–91

freedom of speech
campaign contributions and 46–48, 53–56, 59, 64–67
television and 71–72, 78–79, 82–83

Freedom Summer 22

Fulani, Lenora 89

G

Georgia 42, 52, 98–99

Gerry, Elbridge *96*, 97

gerrymandering *96*, 97–98

Goldberg, Jonah 36

Goldilocks analogy 85

Gore, Al 12–18, 37–38, 92

Gore, Bush v. 17

H

Hagelin, John 89

Hand, Learned 86

hanging chads 16–17

Harrie, Katherine 38

Hayward, Allison R. 61

Help America Vote Act fraud and 35, 42–44

as insufficient 32–33, 92
manipulation of 28
overview of 24–25
provisional ballots and 23

Hilliard, Earl 52, 64

Holder, Northwest Austin Municipal Utility District No. 1 v. 28–30, 40

homosexuality 71

Horton, Willie 69–70, 71

I

identification requirements 27

immigrants 27, 32, 35–38

incumbency protection laws 93

Indiana 27, 42

individual contributions 51–53, 55–56, 63–64

Internet 93–97

intimidation 22–23

Israel 52–53

issue ads 72, 74

issue-centered programming 90

J

Jaffe, Erik S. 65–66, 87

Jeffords, James M. *47*

Johnson, Eddie Bernice 53

Johnson, Miller v. 98–99

Johnson, Tim 37

K

King, Martin Luther Jr. *29*

Ku Klux Klan 22, 55, 73

L

labor unions 46, 63, 84

language barriers 27, 37

LaRouche, Lyndon 89

Legal Defense and Educational Fund (NAACP) 28–30
Levy, Robert A. 66, 87
Lhevine, Paul 78
libel 86
Lincoln Bedroom 51–52
lobbying 50. *See also* Soft money

M

Majette, Denise 52, 64
Malkin, Michelle 36, 40–41
Massachusetts 96, 97–98
McCain, John 11, 46, *47*, 50, 77–78, 87
McCain-Feingold Act. *See* BCRA
McConnell, Mitch 58–59
McConnell v. FEC 64, 66, 73, 88
McKinney, Cynthia 27, 28, 52, 64
media 63. *See also* Television
Media Institute 84–85
Meehan, Martin T. *47*
Meub, William 56
Miller v. Johnson 98–99
Minnesota 18–19, *19*, 76, 77
minorities
  barriers to voting and 24–27, *29*, 30
  effect of "winner-take-all" on 100–102
  motivation behind efforts to register 35–38
  online elections and 94
  redistricting and 97–100
Mississippi 22
Missouri 41
money. *See* Campaign contributions
Montana 70–71

Motor Voter law 23, 28, 31, 34–36, 41–43
murders 22
Murdoch, Rupert 84
Murphy, Kathleen 45

N

National Association of Broadcasters (NAB) 90
National Council of La Raza 32–33
National Voter Registration Act of 1993. *See* Motor Voter law
Native Americans 36–37
Natural Law Party 89
New Alliance Party 89
New York Times Co. v. Sullivan 85–87
1984 (Orwell) 82
Northwest Austin Municipal Utility District No. 1 v. Holder 28–30, 40
NRA (National Rifle Association) 82, 84

O

Obama, Barack 11, 36, 40–41
online elections 93–97
Orwell, George 82
out-of-state campaign contributions 52

P

Pacific Legal Foundation 39
packing 97
Palin, Sarah 11
participation, lack of 11–12, 18–20, *19*, 60
pay to play 49
Peirce, Neal 18
Pepper, George 81
Phillip Morris 50
police officers 12–13
political action committees 69

Political Campaign Broadcast Quality Improvements Act 87
political subdivisions 28–30, 40
polls, exit 14
popular vote 92
poverty 24–27, 35–38
preclearance 28–30, 40
proportional representation 101
provisional ballots 23
public service announcement 78
punch card ballots 13–14, 16–17, 26

R

race 11–13, 39, 52–53, 70–71. *See also* Minorities
Randall v. Sorrell 55, 64–65
Red Lion Broadcasting Co. v. FCC 79
Redenbaugh, Russell G. 38
redistricting 97–100
registration 13–14, 21–25, *29*, 31
Republican Party 35–38, 43–44, 46–50
roadblocks 12–13
Roberts, John 40, 65
Rock the Vote 36
Rosenblum, Jonathan 52

S

Samples, John 41, 61, 62–63
Scalia, Antonin 64, 65, 88
Schier, Steven E. 60
Schumer, Charles 32
Segregation Forever 61, *62*
Shays, Christopher *47*
Smathers, George 81

soft money 46, 48–50, 53–56, 59, 61–67
Sorrell, Randall v. 55, 64–65
Souter, David 27, 55–56, 74
South Dakota 36–37
speech, freedom of. *See* Freedom of speech
Stevens, John Paul 99
student loan scam 71
Sullivan, New York Times Co. v. 85–87

T
Taylor, Mike 70–71
television
  Citizens United case and 46, 74, 82–87, 88
  distortion of real issues and 70–74
  free airtime and 76–80, 87–91
  interference with meaningful election coverage and 74–77

regulation as promoting fairness 69–70
regulation of as unconstitutional 81–85
Texas 28–30, 40
Thernstrom, Abigail 38
Thomas, Clarence 65, 67
Thurmond, Strom 61, 62, 89
Transcendental Meditation 89
Tucker, Roberta 12–13, 19
turnout, lack of 11–12, 18–20, *19*, 60
Twelfth Amendment 95
2000 elections 12–18, *15*, 38–39, 92, 93–94
2008 elections 11, 18–19, *19*

U
undue influence 85
unions 46, 63, 84

utility districts 28–30, 40

V
Valeo, Buckley v. 46, 53–54, 64, 66, 72
Ventura, Jesse 76, 77
Vermont 55–56, 65
Video Voter Guide 78
voter registration 13–14, 21–25, *29*, 31
Voting Rights Act 22, 25, 28, 39, 40

W
West, Darrell M. 70
winner-take-all 100–102
Wisconsin Right to Life, FEC v. 73

Y
Yellowtail, Bill 72–73
York, Byron 37

ALAN MARZILLI, M.A., J.D., lives in Birmingham, Ala., and is a program associate with Advocates for Human Potential, Inc., a research and consulting firm based in Sudbury, Mass., and Albany, N.Y. He primarily works on developing training and educational materials for agencies of the federal government on topics such as housing, mental health policy, employment, and transportation. He has spoken on mental health issues in 30 states, the District of Columbia, and Puerto Rico; his work has included training mental health administrators, nonprofit management and staff, and people with mental illnesses and their families on a wide variety of topics, including effective advocacy, community-based mental health services, and housing. He has written several handbooks and training curricula that are used nationally and as far away as the territory of Guam. He managed statewide and national mental health advocacy programs and worked for several public interest lobbying organizations while studying law at Georgetown University. He has written more than a dozen books, including numerous titles in the POINT/COUNTERPOINT series.